KU-791-275

Introduction

This guide will take you to just over 100 projects built in England over the last ten years. It is an expedition – some of the destinations will be familiar, others will be places to which you never intended to go and to which no other guidebook would direct you. When considering the very recent architecture of any country you have to expect to be sent on one or two wild-goose chases. As some of the buildings described here have only *just* been completed they do not yet carry a seal of approval from critics and historians, they are not yet landmarks on any well-trodden architectural path. Some may never attain that status because they do not present themselves in the glamorous, peopleless images in the pages of magazines and coffee-table books, but they are still important as part of the broader picture. Architecture is people, politics, economics, transport, climate, ethics and the ethnic, technology, science, landscape ... but above all, as the architect Cedric Price states, architecture should be *useful*. So, if you are dedicated to seeing this broader picture, be prepared to end up in some remote and unexpected parts of the country – at times you will feel let down, but at other times euphoric.

England is dominated by a political climate that is now almost 16 years old. Margaret Thatcher's Conservative reign was inaugurated in 1979, the fourth term of office, with John Major more precariously enthroned, began in 1992. On a national scale, manufacturing industry has been attenuated to the point of vanishing (particularly evident on the north, with the closure of steel mills, car factories and coal mines, causing unprecedented levels of unemployment). Direct tax cuts and easy credit have fuelled a retail explosion. The more prosperous south witnessed a building boom that has been as disfiguring to the landscape as the dereliction of so many industrial sites in the north. The greatest compromise of all has been in housing, or the lack of it. Tenants have been encouraged

UNIVERSITY OF
WOLVERHAMPTON
KNOWLEDGE · INNOVATION · ENTERPRISE

Harrison Learning Centre
City Campus
University of Wolverhampton
St. Peter's Square
Wolverhampton
WV1 1RH
Telephone: 0845 408 1631
Online Renewals: www.wlv.ac.uk/lib/myaccount

England

Samantha Hardingham
Photographs by Susan E Benn

A guide to recent architecture

● ● ● ellipsis KÖNEMANN

•••

England: a guide to recent architecture

CREATED, EDITED AND DESIGNED BY
Ellipsis London Limited
55 Charlotte Road London EC2A 3QT
E MAIL ...@ellipsis.co.uk
www http://www.ellipsis.co.uk/ellipsis
PUBLISHED IN THE UK AND AFRICA BY
Ellipsis London Limited
SERIES EDITOR Tom Neville
SERIES DESIGN Jonathan Moberly
LAYOUT Pauline Harrison

COPYRIGHT © 1996 Könemann
Verlagsgesellschaft mbH
Bonner Str. 126, D-50968 Köln
PRODUCTION MANAGER Detlev Schaper
PRINTING AND BINDING Sing Cheong
Printing Ltd
Printed in Hong Kong

ISBN 3 89508 283 X (Könemann)
ISBN 1 899858 00 8 (Ellipsis)

Samantha Hardingham 1995

to buy their council homes, but local authorites have been prevented from building more accommodation for rent – funds are being channelled into incentive schemes and housing for sale. Now the rented housing sector faces a further 30 per cent cut in funding, which will also mean cuts in special-needs housing and accommodation for the disabled.

Many of the houses that did get built in the 1980s were embraced more comfortably by the term 'Community Architecture' which suggests a responsible, caring and generally all-encompassing approach to housing and town planning. It actually launched a comeback in this decade with a Hovis world of pushbikes and home-grown sprouts – the Prince of Wales' brainchild, Poundbury village near Dorchester (see page 244).

To understand how the Prince of Wales arrived at Poundbury and why it is a microcosm of a national pattern of urban development we need briefly to trace the history of 'new towns'. Post-war new towns were designed around the flow of cars rather than people. Ebenezer Howard (1850–1928) set out the principles for fourteen garden cities (the best-known being Welwyn Garden City), lowering the density of the urban population and bringing the city to the countryside. Lacking in cultural activity, they tended to become merely overspill housing for the major cities – suburban sprall. However, Milton Keynes (born in 1968) was different. Its consultant planners, Llewelyn-Davies, Weeks, Forestier-Walker and Bor, proposed social and political evolution by recognising that individuals, private companies, sectional interests and community groups would pour vitality into the city. The general arrangement of Milton Keynes was based on the linked ideas of dispersal and ease of movement. Shops, workplaces and homes are all scattered but contained within a loose grid, or net, of one kilometre square units divided by main roads. Local centres are formed at crossroads between neighbourhoods of approximately 5000 inhabitants. Between the roads and the housing there are deep grassy boarders planted with trees to obscure the two- to three-storey buildings. The roads are called boulevards and housing estates have names like Netherfield, Chevalier Grove and The Watlings.

The names conjur up visions of grand stately homes in landscaped grounds. To some extent this is true as inhabitants of semi-detached boxes clad them in stone and adorn them with Victorian coach lamps, and the proud owners of detached 'period homes' surround themselves with infa-red security lights and conceal steel bars within the tastefully leaded windows. Rowan Moore predicts: 'Noddy houses will have to cause as much damage as tower blocks (which they will)' (*Blueprint*, July/August 1989). On the other hand, to its credit, Milton Keynes has been a unique test-bed for energy-efficient buildings – building a variety of dwelling sizes since 1981 which demonstrate the principles of passive solar heat gain in homes and how they could be built on a commercial basis. By 1988, 600 new homes had been built in Energy Park, a project promoted by the Milton Keynes Development Corporation. This body, directly answerable to the government, has subsequently been wound up. Land has been sold on to developers to keep it out of the hands of local councils, making both the commitment to the energy-efficiency programme and any hope of the new town evolving an urban character uncertain. Milton Keynes has survived on a reputation of television adverts – 'a place without conflict, and sometimes even a place without buildings' (Jeremy Melvin, *Architecture Today*, September 1989). This quality, however , does attract companies from Japan and the United States who are already acclimatised to this kind of enviroment.

In his book *A Vision of Britain* (Doubleday, 1989), the Prince of Wales outlines 'a set of sensible and widely agreed rules, saying what people can and cannot do', stressing the need to preserve the character of our towns and cities and the importance of providing an architecture which people really want and which is on a human scale. By this he means recreating a rural collage using images from the past. He managed to revive public interest in architecture but single-handedly muddied the name of the architectural profession so that the conversation became a for-or-against argument rather than a discussion about anticipating problems that might arise in the future.

What HRH chooses to ignore is that society in the 1990s is dominated by the car, not the pony and trap, by shopping malls, not the village shop, and by Nintendo, not playing with a hoop and a stick in the street. Living in a Disney world of mock crofter's cottages is unlikely to stengthen an individual's sense of place, family and role in the community. It only reinforces a fantasy. There is still a gas-guzzling car in the garage, the superstore is the nearest grocer and the multiplex cinema is the temple of entertainment (the first multiplex to be built in this country was The Point in Milton Keynes). The leisure industry has replaced manufacturing. The Metrocentre in Newcastle contains 360 retail outlets and 6000 jobs under one roof in a Mediterranean-style setting – this constitutes a small town (without the housing) which happens to be owned by the chairman of the town's football team, Newcastle United. We have adopted business parks, leisure parks and now we are bracing ourselves for commerce parks – retail/business/residential parks – a satellite town by definition.

Amongst the clutter there is an architecture which is peculiar to its location, has been designed for a specific purpose and place in time, and represents an ideology beyond that of making a fast buck. Above all it is an architecture where the architect's head has not been put on the chopping block, but a relationship has evolved between the architect and the client

England: a guide to recent architecture

with the shared pursuit of making a better building, not a nicer building. There are some fine examples of this professional support in England which are not limited to one-off private commissions, in particular Hampshire County Council's outstanding programme of design in its infant, junior and primary schools. Hampshire has a reputation as a leading centre for public architecture. In 1974 he department was transformed from an office of routines and system building into a lively architectural practice – following the appointment of the County Architect, Colin Stansfield-Smith (RIBA Gold Medallist, 1991). This was reinforced by the Leader of the Council, Freddie Emery-Wallis, who had a strong vision and the will to improve the environment in the county encompassing conservation programmes (especially tree-planting), to support the arts and to promote good architecture. Richard MacCormac, in his forward to the book *Schools of Thought – Hampshire Architecture 1974–1991*, says, 'Colin Stansfield-Smith's central vision ... developed an exemplary kind of practice in which invention is tested by critical reviews and intention re-charged. This combination of creative freedom within broadly agreed ideas is extraordinarily difficult to manage. Successfully conducted, it represents a highly significant model of how practice, in either the private or public sectors, should be conducted.'

An oustanding catalogue of new building by distinguished architects can be found in university towns, particularly Oxford and Cambridge, the University of East Anglia and Cranfield University, all of them having benefitted from long-standing support from both private and public sectors. University commissions offer an opportunity to architects to create an ultimately democratic architecture; examples include Cranfield Library by Foster Associates and Cable & Wireless College in Coventry by MacCormac Jamieson Prichard.

A primary source of private-sector patronage which has emerged in recent years is the policy adopted by the J Sainsbury supermarket chain – prominent architects (for example, Terry Farrell, Jeremy Dixon . Edward Jones) are commissioned to design façades to attach to the industrial sheds designed by in-house architects. This is a rapidly growing phenomenon, drawing on the fanatical façadism of the 1980s but without decorating the elevations with post-modern nick-nacks. These buildings are the new local landmarks so they must be flamboyant yet diginified. The way to orientate yourself when you get into unfamiliar territory is to ask where the nearest superstore is (usually just on the edge of town); you can leave your car there and venture into the pedestrianised centre.

Beneath this amorphous layer is a catalogue of exceptional one-offs. The buildings that have been chosen are not necessarily competition or award winners (but perhaps some of them should be). They are unique either for their advancement of structural or materials technology (like the Glass Pavilion in Dudley), for their contribution to the regeneration of a community (the National Cycling Centre in Manchester), or not, (the Doncaster Dome), or they trace a particular architect's pattern of work, for example, the many projects included from Michael Hopkins & Partners.

One thing that they have in common is that they are each representative of an architecture that is peculiar to England, its landscape and climate. Many of our architects look abroad for significant commissions but some of the work in this book shows that there is still much to be investigated, even if it is on a small scale and with a limited budget. However, the bigger projects are still out there waiting … to be swept up by the Millenium Commission.

Using this book

As you can see from the map there are big blank areas where there are apparently no contemporary buildings – this is not strictly true. It has not been possible to include *every* built project in this country in the book, and after long deliberation I decided that I wouldn't want to send readers off on long journeys to see indifferent buildings. But let me know if I've missed out something significant; I would be glad to be proved wrong.

As far as navigating through the rest of the book, each entry has a precise address and directions from the nearest main road (motorway or A-road) where possible. If you are in any doubt, either telephone the reception of the building in question or the local tourist information bureau for help. Good luck.

Acknowledgements

This book was made possible by enthusiastic architects, helpful librarians and regional planning departments, good journals, a very patient photographer, an even more patient editor, my long-suffering friend Adam for a barrage of caffeine and boundless humour, and particularly my dear husband Willy for charm, unfailing encouragement and yes … *more* fantastic talk about architecture.
SH February 1995

1 Lancashire,
   Tyne and Wear,
   West Yorkshire
2 Derbyshire,
   South Yorkshire
3 Greater Manchester,
   Cheshire,
   Merseyside
4 Warwickshire,
   Leicestershire,
   Nottinghamshire
5 Cambridgeshire,
   Bedfordshire
6 Norfolk,
   Suffolk,
   Essex
7 Berkshire,
   Wiltshire,
   Gloucestershire
8 Oxfordshire
9 Dorset, Devon,
   Cornwall
10 Avon
11 Hampshire
12 Kent, Sussex,
    Surrey
13 London

Lancashire, Tyne and Wear

Locomotive Maintenance Workshops
Preston

It is clear why this building was winner of the Structural Brickwork Award for 1986. As its name suggests, it is a shed for carrying out repairs on locomotives, but the architect has created a small temple for trains. Like a chapel carved out of brick, it is oblong in plan with a curved apsidal end, and windowless except for skylights in the roof. The exterior elevations are articulated by blind brick arches and round extractor fans instead of windows. The flat end is the entrance for the trains, the tracks penetrating the interior through roller shutter doors. This elevation is surmounted by a pediment adorned (like the decoration of a cathedral's west end) with a central rose extractor fan. The curved end contains a small doorway which leads into the pulpit office, contained in a glass box overlooking the interior of the workshop.

STRUCTURAL ENGINEER Roger Hetherington & Associates
CLIENT Preston Borough Council
SIZE 396 square metres
CONTRACT VALUE £310,000
GETTING THERE from Preston follow signs to the docklands, past a big Morrison's store. Follow the road round along the River Ribble; Chain Caul Road is a turning to the left
ACCESS limited

Lancashire

Brock Carmichael 1985

Brock Carmichael 1985

The Pepsi Max Big One
Blackpool

This is the tallest, fastest rollercoaster in the world. It is made from 2000 tonnes of structural steel and a further 250 tonnes of tubular steel running track, made by British Steel Tubes and Pipes at Corby and supplied and erected by Watson Steel. It rests on almost 1300 pile foundations, took two years to build and stands 20 metres taller than Nelson's Column in Trafalgar Square. From the highest point, the drop has an angle of 65° which allows cars to reach a speed of 85 mph. At this speed passengers are carried a mile in two minutes. Think what this could mean if one were to be installed as a transport system in London: commuters could reach Canary Wharf from Charing Cross Station within 10 minutes – they would just have to remember not eat breakfast first.

The scale of the structure is something to be reckoned with. When a sea fog rises the summit is obscured by clouds like the peaks of a mountain range, but on a clear day the track is scrawled like the printout from a seismograph across Blackpool's skyline. At approximately seven-minute intervals there is an eery calm as the cars crawl up the steep climb, to be catapulted over the other side to a chorus of delighted and terrified screams.

ENGINEERING CONSULTANT Allott and Lomax
CLIENT Blackpool Pleasure Beach Ltd
SIZE 72 metres at its highest point and 1500 metres from start to finish on a 17-hectare site
CONTRACT VALUE £12 million
GETTING THERE on the promenade of the Blackpool Pleasure Beach
ACCESS open

Lancashire

Arrow Dynamics, USA 1994

Lancashire

Arrow Dynamics, USA 1994

George Fox Building and Pendle College

Lancaster University

The George Fox Building and Pendle College are prominent new buildings on the Lancaster University campus. The first, a mixed teaching/office/residential building, was described by *Building* magazine as 'an ingenious … model university building for the 21st century'. 118 en-suite bedrooms, a 350-seat lecture theatre, two 120-seat seminar rooms and two 50-seat seminar rooms, a floor of academic offices and a bistro.

The entrance is defined by a deep forecourt which focuses on a glazed gallery/corridor at first-floor level above wide centrally located doorways. The gallery displays a long wall-hung painting and a route from one side of the building to the other. The circular entrance lobby has a terrazzo floor and glass roof lantern above, suspended by a heavy steel truss (like bicycle spokes). This is a transitional space between lecture room and the bistro. The latter is glazed on two sides and set into the corner of the main façade. Study rooms and offices on the upper floors look inwards on to the top of the lantern and have views on the perimeter of the building of the rest of the campus. Lecture and seminar rooms are on the ground floor at the rear of the building with no passing routes outside so that the limited views out are not distracting.

Pendle College provides accommodation for students in four-storey blocks set around three courtyards with a freestanding commonroom/bar building in one of the courtyards. The plan of each floor is designed to 'provide optimum social grouping balanced with security and comfort'. There are 464 rooms in groups of eight with a shared kitchen/sitting room which projects from the elevation into the courtyard to punctuate between the blocks and to attract more natural light into these rooms. The perimeter elevations echo this punctuation with projecting

Shepheard Epstein Hunter 1993

Shepheard Epstein Hunter 1993

stair towers between blocks. Wooden pergolas are attached to the courtyard elevations but nothing has chosen to grow here.

The commonroom building, like a seaside pavilion, is curved in plan with a glazed west-facing front opening on to steps and the garden court. Inside it has been filled with student bar mock-Victorian pub furniture and carpet which seems to have been treated with due respect. One of the residential wings extends eastwards and turns a corner to wrap around Grizedale College. The elevated rooms have a stunning view of the Lancashire countryside. On the ground floor, recessed from the main façade to form an arcade, are amenity rooms such as the launderette, offices and food court. 'Grizzly's cafe' offers microwaved cheeseburgers in a unforgivingly strip-lit bare room with bolted-down furniture.

The arcade continues to form a link with the rest of the campus and a route past the George Fox Building on your right.

STRUCTURAL ENGINEERS George Fox Building, Harris and Sutherland; Pendle College, George Hutchinson Associates
CLIENT Lancaster University
SIZE George Fox Building, 6800 square metres approx.; Pendle College, 11,400 square metres approx.
CONTRACT VALUE George Fox Building, £4 million; Pendle College, £5.5 million
GETTING THERE follow signs to the University from the centre of Lancaster; buildings are marked on campus map in visitors' car park
ACCESS limited

Lancashire

Shepheard Epstein Hunter 1993

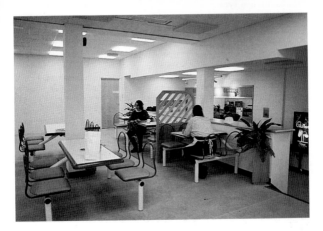

Lancashire

Shepheard Epstein Hunter 1993

Royal Quayside Wet 'n' Wild Waterpark
Newcastle upn Tyne

This is part of a massive 80-hectare plan for the redevelopment of the dockyards – a scenario familiar throughout Great Britain. Here the challenge set by the Urban Development Corporation is the transformation of industrial warehouses, storage yards and ferry terminals into leisure facilities for the 1990s.

The main structure is elegant, flamboyant and expressive. The form and aesthetic of the steel structure borrows from Newcastle's heritage as a shipbuilding city – vast curved steel beams form the skeleton of the canopy, like the ribs of a ship's hull, cradled in the palms of heavy steel columns (pinjoints placed off-centre), with a lightweight roof decking. The wave formation surges above the industrial wasteland and balances delicately on its glazed underbelly and glass with brick base north-facing frontage, the south end sweeping upwards like a flick in the tail to form a brise soleil over the south-facing glazed elevation.

The front elevation is distinguishable by the tornado water ride; two 60-metre braided flumes (water chutes). A glass-block tower attached to the north-east corner of the main shed acts as a beacon for the building at night and is a run-out for some of the green spaghetti flumes which have extruded themselves like innards from the main pool area. Especially effective at night with the dramatic external lighting, bodies fly by in mid-air. Services such as toilets, bars and kitchens are stacked against the brick wall on the first-floor entrance level and a café runs around the poolside on a series of terraces.

The fourteen rides inside include a 110-metre-long 'lazy river', three waterfalls, a wave canyon, a swim-through cave and the first 'white-knuckle twister' flume ride in Great Britain. The main shed is open in parts to draw in cold air in order to circulate fresh air throughout the

Tyne and Wear

FaulknerBrowns 1993

Tyne and Wear

FaulknerBrowns 1993

humid interior.

This is no ordinary swimming pool, it is leisure being touted on an industrial scale, a major new facility targeted at the entire regional community. However, high admission prices (as at the Doncaster Dome) will allow in only the more affluent families in the area, when such a popular form of relaxation should be available to anyone. The architecture suggests this but company concerns do not.

STRUCTURAL ENGINEER Cundall Johnston & Partners
CLIENT Tyneside Waterparks Ltd
CONTRACT VALUE £7.5 million
GETTING THERE The Royal Quays are on the north bank of the River Tyne between Newcastle and the North Sea. The Waterpark stands at the landward gateway to the site
ACCESS open

Tyne and Wear

FaulknerBrowns 1993

Tyne and Wear

Derbyshire and South Yorkshire

Don Valley Athletics Stadium
Sheffield

Don Valley Stadium was the first purpose-built athletics stadium in the country. It was part of the huge push to provide first-rate sports facilities for the World Student Games (second only in size to the Olympic Games) hosted by Sheffield in 1991. Other projects that have been realised as part of the £111 million scheme are the Ponds Forge International Sports Centre, a Supertram transport system (still under construction), an indoor arena, a pool at Hillsborough, and the refurbishment of the Hyde Park flats (soon to be demolished) as accommodation for competitors.

Once a thriving steel town, Sheffield grew fat on heavy industry, beginning in the 18th century with the discovery of silver plating and steel manufacturing in clay crucibles, and becoming world famous for its cutlery. But in recent years the Lower Don Valley has become an industrial graveyard. In the 10 square miles of the Lower Don Valley itself 35,000 jobs have been lost in the last decade. Disused steelworks and other redundant industrial sites are now being revived by the leisure and service sectors in order to find a new economic identity – the Student Games has obviously given the area a tremendous boost.

The stadium was built on the site of an abandoned steelworks at Attercliffe in an artificial bowl created to provide ideal conditions for breaking world records. The ground level was lowered by 4–5 metres and banked up all around the 400-metre track and soccer pitch. The design of the stand puts into practice the recommendations of the Taylor Report (commissioned after a disastrous incident at Hillsborough Football Ground where a crush occurred on the standing terraces and spectators were caged in, unable to escape on to the pitch; there were many fatalities). The stand is a series of yellow-painted steel A frames with a lightweight translucent membrane roof. It seats 10,000 and there is uncovered

South Yorkshire

Design and Building Services, Sheffield City Council 1990

South Yorkshire

Design and Building Services, Sheffield City Council 1990

seating for 30,000. The bases of the A frames, inside the pavilion, create an 85-metre span which accommodates an indoor running track and drug-testing facilities. The entrances are, again, defined by the spaces between the A frames, their huge legs puncturing the main concourse. 6000 square metres of canopy roof are made of Teflon-coated glassfibre. It is supported by the upper part of the yellow structure, a series of Vierendeel ladder masts and cantilevered ladder trusses which support the fabric from above, giving an unobstructed view from the seats.

There are similarities with the construction technique employed at the Mound Stand, Lords Cricket Ground by Michael Hopkins & Partners, although the scale and quality of the materials used are appropriate to each site – here the steelwork is suitably exaggerated.

The stadium is a remarkable achievement, not only as a terrific construction but also because it received absolutely no government funding – the whole scheme received a combination of private-sector support and a trust was set up to own the facilities responsible for financing the pools and arena.

South Yorkshire

PROJECT MANAGER David Whitaker
STRUCTURAL ENGINEER Anthony Hunt Associates
CLIENT Sheffield for Health Limited
CONTRACT VALUE £25 million
GETTING THERE A57, Worksop Road, Sheffield
ACCESS open when in use

Design and Building Services, Sheffield City Council 1990

South Yorkshire

Design and Building Services, Sheffield City Council 1990

Ponds Forge International Sports Centre

Sheffield

Sited strategically next to the Sheffield bus and coach stations, the Ponds Forge pool has taken on Coliseum status – it is a new facility for the local population with international status. The building has created a focus for the city that isn't a shopping centre (this region is famous for the biggest malls in the country and one of the highest unemployment rates). It boasts an Olympic-size competition swimming pool, a leisure pool with fountains, waterfalls and flowing river, a diving pool and dry sports hall. In the foyer area are a cocktail bar and a self-service restaurant. The site is on top of disused mines about 25–30 metres below ground level and culverts 5 metres below ground which carried water from the River Sheaf. These all had to be excavated and filled in – during the process an 85-tonne anvil block, once used for steelmaking, was unearthed and now stands as a monument to the city.

Ignoring the anonymity of the granite-clad exterior (its most striking feature is the flared glass wall surrounding the 'fun' pool) and passing quickly through the double-height foyer space, beyond the double doors, you will reach the main pool. It measures 50 x 25 metres and has two floating floors, enabling areas to be cordoned off for training and aerobics. Two stainless-steel mobile bulkheads further subdivide the pool. At the far end, the diving pool has an underwater system which agitates the surface so that divers can estimate their distance from impact (the top board is 10 metres high). A cushion of giant air bubbles can be released from the bottom of the pool to soften landings during training. There is seating for 3000.

The whole area is covered by a 54 x 84-metre clear-span roof, weighing 400 tonnes and resting on just eight supports. The barrel steelwork roof

South Yorkshire

FaulknerBrowns 1988–90

South Yorkshire

FaulknerBrowns 1988–90

replicates a Norman-style roof pattern of cross-ribs but without the heavy cross-vaulting. It is made up of a web of cross-rib trusses and diagonal infill grillage which meet at cast pin-jointed nodes, all covered in aluminium roof cladding. The supports are A-frame concrete piers.

Both pool areas are particularly impressive in contrast to the unfortunately ostentatious/obstreperous treatment of the foyer area which is now full of hessian partitions displaying art competitions and aerobics-class information. The cocktail bar is draped in 1980s' over-styled light fittings and awkwardly shaped tables in black and fake-walnut finishes, and sited so that only the vaguely partitioned heavy-smokers' end gets a view of the 'fun' pool.

The self-service restaurant is equally disenchanting, with an all-pervading stench of school dinners and motorway café decor. A golden opportunity to entice the exhausted swimmers with hot chocolate and fresh doughnuts has been missed.

South Yorkshire

STRUCTURAL ENGINEER Ove Arup & Partners
CLIENT Sheffield for Health Limited
SIZE pool hall is 5400 square metres
CONTRACT VALUE £41 million
GETTING THERE next to the bus station, Sheaf Street
ACCESS open

FaulknerBrowns 1988–90

David Mellor Factory
Hathersage

This round factory building sits like a small fortress surrounded by a moat (the gutter) in a beautiful wooded enclave. Its circular plan was derived from the existing concrete slab – the remains of a gasometer – on the site. The construction and materials employed in the new building (stone walls and cast-iron roof trusses) were also inspired by the industrial buildings that once stood here. Other contributing factors to the design and choice of materials were the climate (severe), a low-budget, and the location, an area controlled by the Peak Planning Board which requires that new buildings respect the local vernacular. David Mellor is one of the last manufacturers of cutlery in the Sheffield area, once the national home the industry.

A reinforced-concrete disk was cast on top of the slightly smaller existing foundations. Solid walls are faced with stone, according to planning requirements. There are no window apertures, simply four sets of glass double-doors at 12, 3, 6, and 9 o'clock, defined by concrete quoining.

The roof is undoubtedly the most impressive part of the scheme. It is made up of tubular steel trusses restrained by adjustable tie rods at the lowest perimeter and prevented from twisting at the top by a tubular steel ring just below the central lantern. The steelwork is covered by five tiers of plywood boxes that hook on to the steel tubes. Each box is open at the top and bottom edges to create a ventilation channel so that the exterior lead roof lining does not corrode, and to provide a layer of insulation. The central lantern, which provides much of the natural light for the interior, is supported by a central rod and tied to the edges by radiating spoke rods. The entire roof floats above the circular wall on a continuous glazed strip, inserted beneath the eaves.

Michael Hopkins & Partners 1988

Michael Hopkins & Partners 1988

There is a point to be made about the exceptional architect/client relationship that obtained throughout this project. Much of the building work was carried out by the client's own workforce. They cast the concrete quoins and padstones used in the walls, put down the concrete floorslab, undertook masonry work and constructed the plywood boxes, the most arduous task as the 480 boxes had to be made to five different tapering sizes. The robust factory contrasts beautifully with the fineness of the product being manufactured inside. This is an intimate building that oozes personality.

STRUCTURAL ENGINEER Whitby & Bird
CLIENT David Mellor
GETTING THERE go to the village of Hathersage from Sheffield on the A625 (approximately 20 miles west), turn left at the George Inn, under the railway bridge; the entrance is a few metres down on the left
ACCESS open to the public

Derbyshire

Michael Hopkins & Partners 1988

Derbyshire

Michael Hopkins & Partners 1988

The Doncaster Dome

Doncaster sits on one of the largest coalfields in the world, but by the early 1980s the industry, and the jobs of 70 per cent of the working population, had been destroyed. The leisure industry was introduced to restore the rapidly declining image of the town. The site was a 320-acre redundant airfield lying between Doncaster racecourse, Doncaster Rovers Football Club and a nature reserve. It is now a semi-oasis of entertainment featuring an Asda Superstore (with impressive 'A'sda-shaped glass roof), a ten-screen MGM cinema, a bowling alley, and the Doncaster Leisure Dome. These disparate parts strewn across the airfield are linked by a series of small roundabouts – a joy-rider's paradise (I witnessed my first real joy-riding incident here).

I single out the Doncaster Dome because it not only received a commendation from the Royal Institute of British Architects Yorkshire Region White Rose Awards in 1991 (the aim of which is to promote the design skills of architects), but because of the kind of building it claims to be. A brief description from the architect describes the programme: 'The objective was to investigate the potential this site had for a new "leisure-led" park which would act as a catalyst for the economic and qualitative regeneration of the surrounding area. The site strategy was to create a series of landscape layers responding to the northern boundary adjacent to the racecourse (manicured – man in control of nature) and the southern boundary adjacent to the nature reserve (chaos – nature in an entropic state).'

Inside on the north side is the beer-soaked carpeted bar with neon trim (one critic described the carpets as 'migraine-inducing') – man in control of nature; on the south side is the entrance to the auditorium where performers from every walk of life appear, from the Russian Army Cavalcade to the Chippendales – nature in an entropic state. In between there

FaulknerBrowns 1991

South Yorkshire

FaulknerBrowns 1991

is an ice-rink complete with surrounding Alpine scenes (blotting out the joy-riders outside), a leisure pool with waterfalls and jacuzzis, and a health club.

Families of intrepid ice skaters, athletes with super-toned bodies, and beer-bellies have all been transported to this out-of-town/out-of-mind centre to eat bad food and forget about what day or time of year it is. I write in the name of sociability, a sense of occasion and spontaneity. Leisure parks have created a new kind of meeting place where anyone of any age can go but the quality of the experience is hampered by extortionate entrance fees (ruling out a large proportion of the local population which the Dome should attract and which would benefit most from the facilities – the young and the unemployed). The quality and type of food available, the activities on offer leave little to the imagination; you can skate faster, swim until your fingers shrivel and play Mortal Kombat until your eyes go square, and you are still no more aware of where or how you are. Spare us the candy-striped cladding and granite lining. There is nothing about the function of the building which bears any relationship to its surroundings – the quasi-architectural pointers are there to make it look like a building … but it is not.

South Yorkshire

CLIENT Doncaster MBC
SIZE 15,100 squre metres
CONTRACT VALUE £18,923,400 including external works
GETTING THERE A18 to Armthorpe and signs to the racecourse and multiplex cinema
ACCESS open

FaulknerBrowns 1991

South Yorkshire

FaulknerBrowns 1991

The Henry Moore Institute
Leeds

Henry Moore attended art school in Leeds – he would have spent some of his time in the Leeds City Art Gallery (built by George Corson in 1888). A bridge now links the old and new buildings at first-floor level. The Henry Moore Institute provides a unique centre in Europe for the display, study and promotion of sculpture, and includes one of the first galleries to be designed in Europe exclusively for sculpture. The space is spread over four floors in three converted 19th-century wool merchants' offices.

The existing buildings are domestic in scale and character, expressed in the elevation on Cookridge Street, whereas the new elevation onto The Headrow expresses a minimal sculptural idea more in tune with the function of the institute. The Headrow elevation forms the main entrance to the galleries, taking the form of a mechanical repetition of flights of steps generated as the ground falls away across the frontage, set against a sheer black granite vertical plane. The black wall is like a slice through a sculpture or party wall of a building, as if revealing a profile which is never usually visible; five windows notched out of the top and the front door spliced though, off centre, create a refreshingly abstract section of the building. The wall has a tremendous monumentality; the granite has been used in its various natural forms. Vertical grained surfaces are polished and the horizontal grained surfaces are all 'flamed', making a contrasting rough texture. The elevation created by the double-height main gallery, which has filled the courtyard to Alexander Street, is a grid of bronze frames filled with oak and obscured glass with giant doors to allow large sculptures to be moved in and out.

A shallow stepped corridor leads to the foyer and galleries. The interior does not suffer from any mouldings or skirting boards. The concertina stairs, with dividing sand-blasted glass screen, leading up to the library

West Yorkshire

Jeremy Dixon . Edward Jones in association with BDP 1993

West Yorkshire

Jeremy Dixon . Edward Jones in association with BDP 1993

and study rooms on the upper floors provide enough texture to contrast with the simplicity of the rest of the spaces. A fabulous natural luminosity fills the main gallery space which still maintains the feeling of an internal courtyard. The upper floors are heavily carpeted and insulated from external noise, creating a conveniently studious atmosphere.

The caked-on black façade forms the perfect neutral backdrop to the predominantly red-brick Victorian architecture of Leeds, at the same time reminding us how much of that red brick was once caked in soot.

West Yorkshire

STRUCTURAL ENGINEER Whitby & Bird
CLIENT The Henry Moore Foundation
SIZE 6500 square metres
CONTRACT VALUE £3.2 million
GETTING THERE on the corner of Cookridge Street and The Headrow
ACCESS open Monday to Saturday, 10.00–17.30

Jeremy Dixon . Edward Jones in association with BDP 1993

West Yorkshire

Jeremy Dixon . Edward Jones in association with BDP 1993

The Corn Exchange
Leeds

There have been two impressive retail restoration/developments in the centre of Leeds in recent years, the Victoria Quarter and the Corn Exchange, transforming a considerable part of the city.

Leeds first came to prominence in the 17th century as a cloth-marketing centre but it has been hard hit by post-war decline. Planning policies were consequently directed towards offices, public institutions, university buildings, government departments and shopping centres. The city centre displays a catalogue of shopping-centre styles over the ages: the Merrion Centre (1962–65) by Gillinson Barnett & Partners, the Bond Street Shopping Centre (c 1970) by John Burton & Partners, the St John's Centre (mid 1980s) and Schofield's Centre by Crampin and Pring (late 1980s).

The Victoria Quarter was built in 1900 by Frank Matcham (famous as architect of the Coliseum, English National Opera's home in London). The 30,500-square-metre site, owned by Prudential, has been developed by Derek Latham and Associates on a budget of £6.5 million. The Victorian wood and glass shop frontages have been lovingly restored and many of the original types of trade, such as the black pudding shop, still survive alongside gentlemen's outfitters. The whole area is called a 'quarter' because the edges have been left undefined to blend into the rest of the city, unlike an enclosed shopping centre. The central street is covered by a modern steel and glass roof which floats freely above the building fabric, with a 2500-square-metre stained-glass roof window by Brian Clarke.

The Grade 1 listed Corn Exchange was designed by Cuthbert Brodrick (the architect of Leeds Town Hall) in 1861 for the viewing and trading of corn kernels. It cost £360,000 to build. The plan and domed roof derive from an awkwardly shaped site and the need to admit the maximum amount of natural, undazzling, shadowless north light throughout the

West Yorkshire

John Lyall Architects 1990

year to facilitate the viewing of the minute kernels. The roof is made of timber, iron and a combination of opaque and clear glass. The last forms a rectangular band on the south-east side and a central elliptical top light – all of this has been replaced with polycarbonate panels.

The interior space is completely open with a perimeter mezzanine which once led on to offices, now shop units. All of the wrought-iron work and timber flooring has been restored.

The only major alteration to the interior is the 15-metre hole which has been cut into the ground floor in order to make use of the basement area as a food court and create a sweeping double stairway between the floors. The main ground floor area is occupied by an open exhibition space with flexible exhibition stands and is still a stage for the corn tables – once a week in summer, Yorkshire farmers and corn merchants meet to bargain and trade their annual crop.

The building is stocky and its outward appearance is one of indestructibility. The external walls are diamond-shaped rusticated stonework decorated with gutsy garlands and a clock over the main entrance.

Nearby on Crown Street is Third White Cloth Hall, another retail project for the same client and by the same architect, John Lyall. Restored and converted to the tune of £700,000, it is a fine Victorian warehouse with new steel mezzanine structures inserted.

STRUCTURAL ENGINEER White Young
CLIENT Speciality Shops Developments Ltd
SIZE 5000 square metres
CONTRACT VALUE £2.3 million
GETTING THERE Crown Street, Leeds
ACCESS open

West Yorkshire

John Lyall Architects 1990

John Lyall Architects 1990

Alfred McAlpine Stadium
Kirklees, Huddersfield

This stadium is second in size only to Wembley and the plan is to include a multi-screen cinema, bowling alley and theme pub. Presently it seats approximately 16,000 in a three-sided stadium with an eventual capacity of 25,000–28,000 on all four sides. The stadium was built alongside the River Colne to replace Huddersfield's former football ground in response to the disasters that had occurred at Bradford, Heysel and Hillsborough and the Taylor Report which required soccer stadia to be all-seater. The architect's brief was to provide a 25,000 all-seater stadium and to provide leisure facilties that would enhance and expand the life span of the whole complex. What they have produced is a prototype for 'a stadium for the '90s'. It is owned by a company comprising the local council, the football club and Huddersfield Rugby League Club, so is very much a local and national landmark – Huddersfield Town is one of several the smaller football clubs in this region to set their sights a little higher than the shed grounds of the less ambitious clubs, and as a result they have an architectural and engineering milestone on their hands.

The plan is based on a maximum viewing distance of 150 metres from the four corners of the pitch, producing (ultimately) four orange-segment shaped stands and an oval plan overall. The roof (made of blue profile-metal sheets) over each stand is supported from above by an arched truss (now known as banana trusses). This approach to the structure enables the roof canopy to be very deep (increasing good sightlines) because there is no forest of columns or too much strain put on the cantilever alone. The trusses are made up of a tubular steel prismatic structure – the largest element spans 140 metres. They were constucted in sections and bolted together prior to lifting them into position on the supports, attaching them with pin connections. The trusses seem to grow out of reinforced-

West Yorkshire

Lobb Partnership 1994

concrete finger supports or thrust blocks which also provide a base for the stadium's floodlights. The control centre crouches on fingers in the north-west corner, housing security teams during matches.

The sheer magnitude of the stadium can be experienced from various points in and around the site. From a distance the structure is an elegant set of curves in the landscape, whereas standing beneath the corner finger supports is like being inside the base of the Eiffel Tower. A breathtaking view of the pitch is from the approach into the car park behind the south stand. Climbing up the steep driveway you finally hit the brow of the hill and there lying before you is the stadium. At this point you are at roof level and so close to it that the banana trusses take on a bridgeing role, leading the eye into the valley which slopes away to the north and views of Huddersfield beyond. At the same time the south stand roof frames a view down on to the pitch and forms a grand arch over the stairway access which descends into stands. However, only a few people know how it looks when emerging from the players' tunnel in the Riverside Stand – probably the most thrilling and enormous view of all.

STRUCTURAL ENGINEER YRM Anthony Hunt
CLIENT Kirklees Stadium Development Ltd
SIZE 20 hectares
CONTRACT VALUE £2 million, 10-year sponsorship deal between Alfred McAlpine (the contractors) and Kirklees Stadium Development
GETTING THERE follow signs from town centre to Kirklees Stadium
ACCESS open during matches, limited at other times

West Yorkshire

Lobb Partnership 1994

West Yorkshire

Lobb Partnership 1994

Fountains Abbey Visitors' Centre
Studley Royal Park, Ripon

Fountains Abbey was built 700 years ago by dissident monks as a place of refuge and retreat. It stands in a tranquil, ravine-like valley. The top of the tower emerges above the trees as you approach down the hillside and you begin to appreciate the soaring scale of the abbey and its surrounding buildings with the valley and river running behind into the distance. The perpendicular tracery in the abbey windows emphasises the fragility of the ancient ruin, but also its lastingness. It is a peaceful and magical place; the light has an unusual feathery texture, a mixture of mist and sunshine.

Further down the valley are the beautifully landscaped gardens of 18th-century Studley Royal Park – water and woods scattered with neo-classical follies. There is one small shelter set high up in the woods which looks back along the valley with the abbey at the end. The view is timeless. For these reasons this is the most visited of all National Trust properties – 300,000 people a year come here. And for the same reasons the National Trust wanted to temper the effects that such a mass of people might have on the site, by moving all unsightly amenities away from the abbey, and by enriching the visitor's experience by interpreting more of the story of the site. The response was this visitors centre at the site entrance, a good ten-minute walk from the abbey itself.

The siting of the visitors' centre is particularly uninspired – on the brow of the hill with an initial vista of the abbey turrets through the wooden loggia entrance and diagonally across the central courtyard, but there is no sense of place from anywhere else within the building. In a place famous for its imaginatively yet discreetly sited follies, which take full advantage of the surrounding landscape and create a new landscape at the same time, this addition seems brutish.

West Yorkshire

Edward Cullinan Architects 1993

West Yorkshire

Edward Cullinan Architects 1993

The building aims to interpret the rugged Yorkshire landscape by using traditional and tactile materials– wood, slate and stone – and spatially by making overlapping and interpenetrating spaces. This is expressed externally by the double-curved roof. The basic plan is two single-storey L-shaped buildings around a courtyard. One accommodates the restaurant, kitchen, and lavatories; the other houses the shop, an exhibition space and auditorium. The steel framework is exposed with specially designed brackets, cleats and extended guttering (a Cullinan trademark). A dry-stone wall base acts as a rainscreen. The exterior is clad with alternating cedar and glass panels.

The logic of the structure is clearly demonstrated by the canopy that runs around the perimeter of the courtyard – lead sheeting on timber boards, laid on joists, on steel angles, on cleats welded to tapered cantilevers, supported by round columns. The interior is insulated by exposed plywood sheeting. The first grating detail is introduced here – a series of brightly painted 2 x 4 wooden strips are fixed to the plywood ceiling to express the presence of hidden joists. The feature is flimsy and lets down the natural ruggedness of the exterior. As in other buildings of this genre, the exhibition space is under-used and simply displays a series of story-telling panels providing no more information or sense of the place than could be found in any pamphlet.

The restaurant is another pitfall – as sophisticated as a motorway self-service cafeteria, smothered in the same superficial ceiling decoration and poorly made plywood lighting panels. The view from here is of a built-up grassy bank. The shop sells the usual National Trust trinkets.

The architect has undoubtedly explored the potential of materials on the exterior, creating dramatic forms and using intriguing methods of construction, but it is also the client's responsibility to allow the architect

Edward Cullinan Architects 1993

West Yorkshire

Edward Cullinan Architects 1993

to define the specific use and maximise the potential of the spaces he creates. A visitors' centre should be a source of information, extending your knowledge of the place that you are visiting. Eating a pre-packed egg-and-cress sandwich and buying a floral toothmug, no matter what the building looks like, is not going to enrich the experience. Siting and the experience offered inside the building should be integral to any visitors'-centre brief.

West Yorkshire

STRUCTURAL ENGINEER Jampel Davison and Bell
CLIENT National Trust
SIZE 500 square metres
CONTRACT VALUE £2.3 million
GETTING THERE 5 kilometres from Ripon, west on the B6265 towards Pately Bridge
ACCESS open 10.00–17.00 every day; closed on Fridays in November, December and January

Edward Cullinan Architects 1993

Edward Cullinan Architects 1993

Merseyside and Manchester

Claverton Court
Chester

One of the few housing projects to be included in the guide, Claverton Court represents an approach widely applied to the smattering of housing schemes built throughout England in recent years. Schemes are designed with a specific market in mind, but standard guidelines are applied so that one house is indistinguishable from another. Claverton Court certainly looks like an old people's home, but it is not just any old people's home. It is a competition- and award-winning home for retired architects.

The two-storey, red-brick building is built in a cresent, the inside curve facing south-west with a conservatory in the middle, and the outer face directed north-east, overlooking the garden and the street. All flats have views in both directions 'to increase social interaction', the architect says.

For a profession whose members are supposed to be visually literate, spatially aware and socially and politically conscious for most of their lives, why should they be 'topped-out' in a vaguely aggrandised, suburban rabbit hutch? What would happen if Norman Foster, Will Alsop, Zaha Hadid and the partners at FaulknerBrowns were sent to spend their twilight years under the same roof? I cannot imagine that they would be resting easy in Parker-Knoll rockers comparing damp-course details – so why should their lesser known colleagues be treated in this way?

STRUCTURAL ENGINEER Roger Hetherington & Associates
CLIENT Architects Benevolent Fund
SIZE 812 square metres
GETTING THERE from the visitors' centre in Chester, over the footbridge, turn right at Victoria Crescent, follow the road around to Queens Park Road, 500 metres round on the left
ACCESS private property – access limited

Cheshire

Brock Carmichael 1984

Cheshire

Brock Carmichael 1984

The Tate Gallery
Liverpool

The Albert Docks is a wonderful site, built in 1846 by Jesse Hartley and the largest group of Grade 1 listed buildings in the UK. They have been redeveloped as part of a regeneration scheme for the city, as a sort of urban/industrial leisure park incorporating the Maritime Museum and involving the reconditioning of surrounding dock apparatus (bridges, lifting devices and pump houses), intermingled with retail space, apartments, a television studio and an art gallery (the Tate). The result is predictably half-hearted.

There is no doubt that the original series of four buildings surrounding the central 'plaza of water' (as Stirling described it) are stunning and create a unique setting. But the ground floor of all four buildings has been linked to form a continuous arcade of card and candle shops, phoney American restaurants and grotesque candy stores punctuated by an excess of unlet space – there are no real resources except for one news-agent. The water plaza is the stage for a moored tugboat/coffee shop and a floating polystyrene model of the UK which is used as a weather map on breakfast television. The Maritime Museum has a bland trad theme-park approach to its depiction of the history of this major port. To sum up, the whole scene serves as a backdrop for the 'Richard and Judy Show', a mid-morning TV chat show, filmed here in Granada's studio.

Tucked in the north-west corner is the Tate Gallery. Its blind façade of bright blue and orange panelling with large double revolving doors and illuminated three-dimensional lettering is set back beneath an arcade of vast cast-iron columns, painted pale terracotta. The smooth panels provide a striking modern contrast to the monolithic, rough-cast iron-and brickwork, but the colour statement is discreet in comparison with the scale of the original buildings. In this way the architect has not

Merseyside

Stirling Wilford & Associates 1988

Merseyside

Stirling Wilford & Associates 1988

attempted to meddle with Hartley's building, he has simply devised a way of inserting modern services into the shallow brick-vaulted warehouse spaces which serve as the galleries. The only other major interventions are the entrance lobby mezzanine and the main stairway and vertical service spine.

The entrance lobby has a stone floor (a continuation from outside) and fair-faced brick walls. A double-curved, blue-clad mezzanine bulges out above your head – this is the café. To the right is the bookshop which makes use of the porthole windows in the façade as its display cases. To the left is an entrance into a double-height ground-floor gallery space and opposite the entrance is an opening leading around a corner to the main staircase. This is the route to the café and mezzanine overlooking the rear ground-floor gallery and to two levels of galleries above. The gallery spaces have low ceilings – shallow brick vaults on a grid of inverted Y-beams on slender cast-iron columns. All the cast-iron elements are painted pale grey. Running longitudinally down the centre of each floor is a duct made from pressed steel and painted pale grey which contains air-conditioning ducts, lighting, a public-announcement system and infra-red lighting. The system is an innovation in the building and was developed by the services engineers Steevson Varming Mularky & Partners with Philips. The vertical service spine running between the floors contains stairs, lifts and all primary services. Parts of the basement and third floor are used as plant rooms. Upper gallery floors are finished in beech and where the columns meet the floor a bronze surround has been set flush with the timber like a porthole opening in the floor.

Deceptively large from the outside, the close grid of columns inside the gallery spaces does not make the rooms ideal for showing large works of art. The gallery is the first in England to be exclusively devoted to

Stirling Wilford & Associates 1988

Stirling Wilford & Associates 1988

modern art and the requirements do not seem to fit well with Hartley's building programme. Stirling was left little option but to intervene as discreetly as possible in order not to interupt the spaces even more. Even so, the ceiling ducts are quite dominant in the rooms.

Stirling was raised in Liverpool – you can see that the original Albert Docks were already very much like a Stirling project. His initial proposal was for an exterior structure to be made of ship's parts, creating a new separate entrance and linked to the main galleries by escalators. This was rejected on grounds of conservation and planning. However, it might have allowed Stirling to approach the circulation of the building in a way that would have made better use of the tight interior spaces and given him the opportunity to develop a sequel to the Clore Gallery in London, completed just two years earlier in 1986.

STRUCTURAL ENGINEER W G Curtin & Partners
CLIENT Trustees of the Tate Gallery
SIZE 12,000 square metres of which 2600 square metres are gallery space
CONTRACT VALUE £9.5 million
GETTING THERE on the north-west corner of the Albert Docks, which can be approached from Strand Street, the main road which runs alongside the Mersey
ACCESS open

Merseyside

Stirling Wilford & Associates 1988

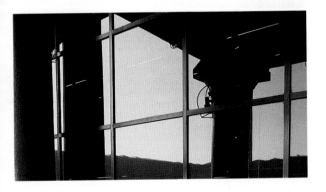

Stirling Wilford & Associates 1988

Merseyside

Aldham Roberts Learning Resources Centre

John Moores University, Liverpool

The architect's concept was the creation of a focal point for the university and a 'gateway' building. Perhaps the former has been achieved; the centre is sited right next to the student union which is an established focus. But the latter seems a little over-stated, as the building is difficult to reach and the approach from the west side is obscured by closely packed streets leading you to the back of the building. Once you do reach it, however, the light shines through the building, lifting it from its austere surroundings – the ruins of St Andrew's Church of Scotland to the west and various grim Victorian buildings and ex-convent gardens to the east.

The glass and white-walled pavilion has a square plan. The east corner has been bitten off to reveal all of the four floors, beginning at lower ground level. A double-curved Planar glass screen seals this three-storey atrium, capped by a space-frame roof structure which projects outside to complete the square again and form an entrance canopy. The reflection of the space-frame in the glazed wall has a honeycomb effect and the swarms of students pouring in and out of the building through the mean central rotating door conjur up the image of a bee-hive rather than a gateway.

Inside the atrium, lean against the polished stainless steel bannister rail and you can feel the building vibrating as people walk up and down the wood-treaded stairs. It is like being inside a musical instrument.

The architects here might have taken note of the visual and organisational clarity of Foster's library at Cranfield (see page 166) which so successfully defines areas for study around the perimeter, with the delicate bookstacks in fixed rows. Here the plan is divided by aisles orientated east–west and north–south, defined by the heavy timber bookstacks

Austin-Smith: Lord, Warrington 1993

which do not reach the ceiling, floating aimlessly in the open-plan floors. Paper labels have been stuck crookedly on the sides and trolleys hover in the aisles.

The ground and lower ground floors are intended as noisier areas – for group studies, computer terminals, quick reference and book issue and return. The upper two floors are quieter areas with dense bookstacks, presently sited towards the centre of the plan with a continuous desk running around the perimeter. The plan is flexible in that the area assigned to bookstacks (a 7.2-metre structural grid – the optimum module for bookstacks and study areas) could be repositioned in the open plan to cope with an increase in material or demand for information-technology resources (presently confined to the ground floor). The controllable artificial lighting also allows for this flexibility.

The ground on the garden side has been cut away to allow natural light to penetrate the lower ground floor; it also helps to integrate the building with its site.

STRUCTURAL ENGINEER Ove Arup & Partners, Manchester
CLIENT John Moores University
SIZE 5700 square metres
CONTRACT VALUE £5 million
GETTING THERE complicated – at the top of Mount Pleasant, opposite the Roman Catholic Cathedral, turn right down Hope Street, past the Everyman theatre. Take a turning on your right; straight ahead is the student union with the back of the Resource Centre on the right
ACCESS visitors are free to wander around the public areas but not inside

Merseyside

Austin-Smith: Lord, Warrington 1993

Watersports Centre, Queen's Docks
Liverpool

Part of Liverpool's Waterfront Area Strategy involved introducing a new building to attract more local residents and schools to participate in water sports. Interest was already there, but the new building, with additional facilities, should enhance the experience. The building is designed to cope with a throughput of 80 people an hour for canoeing, sailing and wind-surfing instruction.

The design philosophy was clearly determined by the siting of the centre, in the water about 15 metres from the quayside. All sides of the building could be used and visitors would immediately engage in the idea of being in the water. A superstructure – twelve columns, each branching out into four arms to support the rectangular truss frames of the canti-levered top deck – stands on a reinforced-concrete deck attached to 900-mm-diameter concrete piles beneath. The raft does not float, it only appears to adjust to the 300 mm change in water level. The two-storey enclosure above is linked to the shore by three walkways, one to the lower boat house deck for parts and two to the upper deck for people. This top deck accommodates clearly defined wet and dry areas, separated by a central access point. Wet areas are at the west end (booking-in, changing and shower rooms, wet-suit store, drying room and staff room) and the dry area is on the east end (offices, shop, lecture room and café).

The whole enclosure is surrounded by a deck which runs around the perimeter, sheltered by the protruding eaves of the shallow curved roof, clad in profiled aluminium, which rests on pin joints on each of the main frames. The enclosure is clad in Western red cedar boarding which will go silver with age. The windows are made from an aluminium and wood composite and interiors are white-painted blockwork with linoleum floors. Two-thirds of the lower deck is enclosed in a galvanised steel mesh

Merseyside

David Marks Julia Barfield Architects 1994

Merseyside

David Marks Julia Barfield Architects 1994

for boat storage; the plant room is clad in profiled aluminium. The transparency of the mesh adds to the lightness of the structure and the fine cast detailing of the branch supports on the columns is reminiscent of the cast-iron elements found in other dockyard buildings, but proportions have been adjusted and shapes refined to avoid pastiche. It is an elegantly functional building, making interesting use of the site without trying to compete with the scale of other dockland constructions.

On the same quay is the Mariners Wharf housing development, a preposterous Po-Mo-meets-the-Mary-Rose development. Profiled Gyproc pillars supporting rough-cast concrete pediments, already stained from dripping water, an assortment of bannister rails slapped across the stair-well windows forming a prominent feature of the front elevation to each block, scaffold poles and heavy-duty cabling employed to make balconies that are too shallow to use – these are just some of the construction delights, the fast-food of building. Best of all is the security lodge which is adorned with such delicately ornate window bars that a small child in a tantrum might be able to pull them off, while the roof is so top heavy with corner tiles that it might just sink under its own weight.

STRUCTURAL ENGINEER Ove Arup & Partners/Loren Butt Consultancies
CLIENT Merseyside Development Corporation
SIZE raft slab 1509 square metres; enclosure 817 square metres
CONTRACT VALUE £1.125 million
GETTING THERE approximately 5 minutes drive east of Albert Docks, turn right at Mariners Wharf, past the Dolby Hotel
ACCESS limited

Merseyside

David Marks Julia Barfield Architects 1994

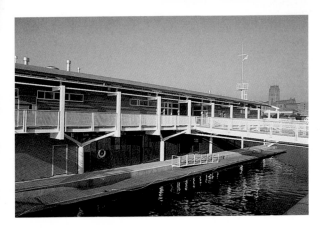

Merseyside

David Marks Julia Barfield Architects 1994

Museum of Science and Industry
Manchester

The Museum of Science and Industry occupies the five 19th-century warehouses and train sheds of Liverpool Road Station, the world's oldest surviving passenger railway station. The buildings are part of the Castlefield Conservation Area, designated because of its importance in the development of transport during the Industrial Revolution. BDP has been involved in the design strategy for the whole project, including conversion of the 1870s' market hall into the Air and Space Gallery, conversionof a series of railway arches into the National Gas Gallery, reconstruction of Grade I listed carriage sheds built in 1830 and conversion of the Lower Byrom Street Warehouse. This last building accommodates the main museum entrance, archives and record centre, shop, educational services such as classrooms and meeting rooms, a café called 'Xpression' and the interactive science centre called 'Xperiment'. As you shall see, the strongest design concept and educational tool is bad spelling.

The four-storey brick warehouse was built in 1880. The conversion involved cutting a vertical slot through the centre of the building and inserting a gently graded zig-zagging steel ramp, forming a new circulation route through four floor levels.

This project is an opportunity lost – no amount of zany names for exhibits and airport cafeteria facilities can make up for the lost beauty, scale and purpose of the original building.

STRUCTURAL ENGINEER BDP
CLIENT Trustees of the Museum of Science and Industry in Manchester
SIZE 3.5 hectares
GETTING THERE on Liverpool Road, off Deansgate
ACCESS open 10.00–17.00, seven days a week

Greater Manchester

Greater Manchester

Castlefield Visitors' Centre and Staffordshire Wharf Outdoor Arena
Manchester

This complex is part of a programme intended to revitalise the existing urban fabric of Manchester, such as bridges and warehouses, and here a piece of unused ground next to the canal. The area of Castlefield, just a five-minute walk from the city centre, is already a well-known tourist attraction with the Museum of Science and Industry over the road, the Granada Television Studio Tour on Water Street, and canal-side walks. The new arena and visitors' centre provide venues for local and national events – 20,000 people gathered here to find out the result of Manchester's bid for the 1996 Olympic Games, which, although it ended in failure, had aleady stimulated the building of some first-rate facilities for a city which has long been in decline.

The visitors' centre is one of the more successful of its kind. It has almost been split down the middle – a lightweight steel and glass pavilion on one side and a white-clad box on the other. The glazed side is the public face, accommodating a full-height exhibition area beneath a curved silver roof. The entrance is at ground level on Liverpool Road but the ground slopes away towards the south so a lower ground-floor level is formed and there is a balcony facing out over the arena. The clad side accommodates offices and public lavatories which can be accessed from outside.

The arena is like a miniature amphitheatre. It is made up of a few simple but well executed elements: a curved terrace of pre-cast concrete seating facing west overlooking an open York-stone stage with granite setts which reaches down to the canalside. The backdrop to this is a rather unfortunate brand-new Lego-brick hotel with red-painted balustrading, but there is a more interesting view to the left underneath the high railway bridges and along the canal. The seating is covered with a modular tensile

DEGW Scotland 1994

DEGW Scotland 1994

canopy, each fabric peak supported by a triangular tubular-steel frame lodged at a tilting angle behind the back row so that it appears to fold up and down. Sadly, the front of the canopy does not extend beyond the second row of seats so the front row gets wet – another half a metre and this would have been covered. Behind the seating on one side and to the sides are low walls of red sandstone. The control room is in a sandstone bunker with the lighting tower above at the centre. The seats on the other side have a background of steeply stepped lawns which adds a striking block of colour to the geometric composition of parts.

This project sets an example for simple, imaginative urban landscaping – there are no hanging baskets and no municipal street furniture. It is a useful empty space in an area where you might least expect it.

Greater Manchester

STRUCTURAL ENGINEER visitors' centre, McLay Collier & Partners; arena, Ove Arup & Partners
CLIENT Central Manchester Development Corporation
CONTRACT VALUE £1.2 million
GETTING THERE on Liverpool Road, off Deansgate
ACCESS open

DEGW Scotland 1994

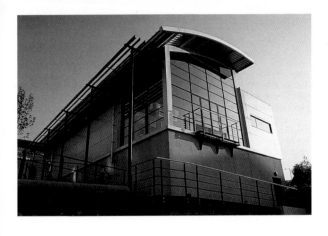

Greater Manchester

DEGW Scotland 1994

The Pump House: People's History Museum

Manchester

Manchester is the United Kingdom's centre for museums covering the social history of working people. On Prince's Street, the National Museum of Labour History is a Labour Party archive, with papers and artefacts such as trade-union banners, posters and pamphlets. The Edwardian Pump House next to the River Irwell has been rejuvenated and adapted to provide a permanent home for the collection as part of the Castlefield Urban Heritage Park.

There are four elements to the design: a reception/shop area, a performance space and coffee shop, the main split-level exhibition space, and a temporary exhibition space at the top. At the entrance, in the former engine hall, a single low partition doubles up as the reception desk on one side and the coffee shop on the other. The high ceilings and tall full-height windows lend themselves to creating the performance space in the centre, punctuated by a brick-clad lift shaft which marks the entrance to the exhibition beyond.

The exhibition gallery is in what was the boiler house. A new mezzanine level has been inserted, hung within the 6-metre-high room by diagonal ties bolted to the original structural beams. The exhibition design itself is by Nigel Simpkins – a series of plywood panels to create corners of rooms and display cases; varying floor levels help to differentiate between different eras and subjects.

The temporary exhibition gallery is up at the top in the old coal store, reached via a new staircase at the rear of the building with a river view through a full-height glazed wall. The stair wall is painted with bold graphics advertising the presence of the museum to the people in restaurants on the opposite river bank.

Greater Manchester

OMI 1993

The main exhibition is fascinating, containing everything from Stanley Matthews' football boots to printed matter from the coal-miners' strike in the early 1980s.

Greater Manchester

STRUCTURAL ENGINEER Buro Happold
CLIENT The National Museum of Labour History
CONTRACT VALUE £1.3 million
GETTING THERE Left Bank off Bridge Street, Manchester
ACCESS during opening hours

OMI 1993

Greater Manchester

OMI 1993

Dry 201
Manchester

Dry 201 was the second in a series of ventures initiated and co-owned by Factory Records (which has since taken on another form) and the band New Order, the first being the Haçienda in Whitworth Street, the best-known night club in Manchester and the launch pad for bands such as the Happy Mondays and the Stone Roses. Both projects were designed by Ben Kelly, a member of the generation of designers that includes Peter Saville and Neville Brody, more familiar for their graphics. 201 was added to the name because Factory Records always assigned a catalogue number to their projects. The café/bar/restaurant was the first of a genre which has flourished in the centre of town, created as a place to hang out in before going clubbing.

The stainless steel bar is 24 metres long, inserted into the deep plan of an old furniture showroom. The 'display' element is still very strong as the full-height front window (spanning two-thirds of the width of the frontage) and wide Japanese oak door lures customers inside as an extension of the pavement. The scale and sense of exterior elements are introduced into the interior in the form of telegraph poles which divide the space longitudinally, between the main bar and diagonal leaning bars on the left and the seating area on the right (furniture is sturdy plywood school desks and stacking chairs). At the back a more enclosed, comfortable seating area is furnished by Jasper Morrison, as is a corner of the front window.

The aesthetic throughout clearly does not want to be labelled – a mix of industrial elements overlaps the elegant shapes of furniture and colours of pigmented and moulded plaster. A Kee-Klamp lighting track over the bar and extending through the front window is adorned with delicate acid-etched glass reflectors, patches of the original timber and terrazzo

Ben Kelly Designs 1989

Greater Manchester

Ben Kelly Designs 1989

floor surfaces remain intact so that (the designer states) new interventions become 'endowed with as much strangeness of presence as possible'. The bar has the capacity to serve up to 500 customers at any one time, is beer soaked but very cosmopolitan.

CLIENT Factory Records/New Order
SIZE 779 square metres (ground floor and basement)
GETTING THERE 28 Oldham Street, east of the town hall, across Piccadilly Gardens
ACCESS open Monday to Sunday

Ben Kelly Designs 1989

Ben Kelly Designs 1989

National Cycling Centre
Manchester

This is the first purpose-built indoor velodrome ('speed track') in Great Britain. It was built as part of Manchester's bid to host the next Olympic Games and provided the opportunity for a derelict area of the city to begin regeneration. The Olympics went to Sydney, Australia but fortunately this facility was completed and will host the 1996 World Cycling Championships. It is now one of six national sports centres.

The building says 'speed' all over. The design emulates the form of the track, oval in plan and streamlined in elevation. It is the shape of a cyclist's helmet hugging the ground, lashed down by a 122-metre clear-span, arched box truss, resting on external concrete thrust blocks that minimise the number of foundations. The arch forms the skeletal backbone of the domed structure (which is constructed of 600 tonnes of steel) and a clerestory over the main arena. Inside, the steel-lattice trusses of the roof structure are set on a constant 13° pitch span, providing a sinuous curve right out to the eaves of the building. The seating bowl below provides for 3500 spectators, with seating on two sides and a continuous concourse all the way around for clear sight lines from almost any point within the arena. Eight entrance and exit points lead spectators directly up to a perimeter concourse on the first-floor level which in turn leads into the main bowl.

Competitors and VIP entrance/exits are at the rear of the building on the ground floor. There is a private concourse beneath, with 360° circulation for competitors, including facilities such as changing rooms, weight-training, physiotherapy and doctors' rooms and a cafeteria for competitors. From here, three tunnels leading into the arena allow smooth access and run off routes, to and from the track.

The 250–metre track was designed by the specialist, Ron Webb. It is made of a single layer of 40 mm square Siberian pine timbers layed on

FaulknerBrowns 1994

FaulknerBrowns 1994

top of timber trusses, each one fabricated individually to accommodate the 12.5° pitch on the straight through to a maximum pitch of 42° on the curves. It is designed to maximise speed with a steeper pitch on the exit of the curve which catapults the cyclist down the straight and the hope is that we shall see many new world records. In the centre is a 40-square-metre semi-sprung floor for sports such as badminton and basketball. Lighting above is to television standards.

The exterior is clad in blue engineering bricks on the lower level and a system of composite panels with a silver micro-profile finish and blue-tinted double glazing reaching up to the eaves. The aluminiumroof covering was erected early on in the construction process so that other stages of building could be done in the dry. Each feature and colour of material contributes to the streamlined form and organic quality of the whole, inside and out. The building sets an excellent standard for what might have been an unchallenging design and build contract. It also signals to the rest of the country that Manchester has the confidence to proceed with its regeneration programme.

STRUCTURAL ENGINEERS AMEC Design and Build Ltd, with Watson Steel (roof steelwork) and C V Buchan (concrete terracing)
CLIENT Manchester City Council, the Sports Council and the British Cycling Federation
SIZE 10,000 square metres
CONTRACT VALUE £9 million
GETTING THERE on the Piccadilly side of Manchester, take the A662 towards Clayton and Beswick on the Ashton New Road, follow along until you see the building on your left-hand side
ACCESS open

Greater Manchester

FaulknerBrowns 1994

FaulknerBrowns 1994

Hanah 1
Irlam, Manchester

Studio BAAD is gaining a reputation for designing and building inventive, modern buildings on a very tight budget – the kind of budget that demands invention because any off-the peg material or fitting is just too expensive. This is the most recent building to be completed by the practice (another significant project is the Simon Jersey office block in the Altham Industrial Estate, Accrington), providing space for storage and associated offices and showrooms for a company that imports gifts (dolls, children's furniture, etc). The client's brief was flexible: the only requirement was as much space as possible for £200,000. The architects proposed a very simple enclosure with a few elaborations to distinguish office from storage areas. They have also endeavoured to make the building stand out as a whole from neighbouring warehouses without going for a cheap and cheerful approach.

The blockwork shell is braced internally with diagonal steel props and clad externally with a silver corrugated-metal skin. In places the metal has been shaved away and clear corrugated plastic is grafted on over internally glazed window openings. However, most of the natural light that infiltrates the building enters through skylights set in three roof domes, creating a cave-like effect. The entrance is formed by a bulge in the east side of the shed, again clad in corrugated metal, but coloured metallic green, painted by a car sprayer. This leads into the reception tower, a fully glazed south-east-facing corner. The glass is flush with the corrugated perimeter walls but the tower protrudes from the rest of the enclosure because of the deep *brise-soleil* shading both sides. The staircase which leads from here up to the offices on the same side of the building is shielded from the noisier storage rooms by a sheer concrete cliff.

Materials were left as installed, without concealing plaster or decora-

Studio BAAD 1994

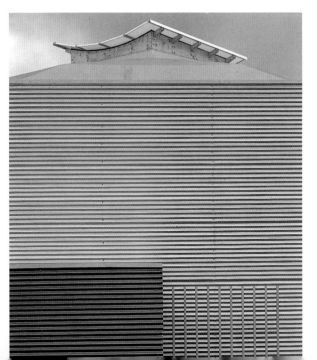

tion. Blockwork, MDF, flakeboard and concrete all achieve what the architects describe as the 'elemental and geological' quality of the building – raw in the most elegantly detailed way.

It is inspiring to see what can be achieved when the uses of a limited range of cheap materials are reinvented, and when sub-contractors are also prepared to rise to a challenge.

Greater Manchester

CLIENT Hanah
SIZE 1000 square metres
CONTRACT VALUE £200,000
GETTING THERE off the M63, follow the A57 to Irlam and then signs for the North Bank Industrial Park. The building is on the right-hand side on Huntsman Drive
ACCESS very limited

Studio BAAD 1994

Greater Manchester

Studio BAAD 1994

Warwickshire, Leicestershire, Nottinghamshire

Cable & Wireless College
Coventry

The Cable & Wireless College is a training and conference centre for company employees and up to 300 company-sponsored students from all over the world. The building is approached from the south side and is perceived as a series of layered wings which peel away from the centre. The base structure is predominantly made of a warm, sandy-coloured concrete with blue tiled roofs, curved like waves breaking over a beach. The deep-plan wings (47.5 metres deep by 70 metres long) accommodate teaching areas, conference rooms, a library and laboratories and are arranged in three parallel lines divided longitudinally by corridors so that the rooms in the centre can be accessed from either side. The rooms themselves are divided by demountable partitions at 4.5-metre intervals. The curves in the roofline create a continuous north-facing clerestory along each line of classrooms, admitting generous amounts of indirect natural light and enabling passive ventilation to be used.

The main entrance is actually via the northernmost wing. This accommodates the reception, administration and dining room in the centre, flanked by living quarters; generally visitors to the east and long-term students to the west. The rooms are arranged in groups of twenty around one staircase; cooking facilities and common rooms are provided in the main body of the building. The corporate message is strong, the focal point of the plan being an ocular courtyard called the 'Eye of Knowledge'. Occupants have to pass through this courtyard to reach any of the other parts of the building. The dining room is located next to the courtyard and is screened by a curved glass wall. The library on a first floor mezzanine level and communal meeting spaces are on the opposite side. From this point there is also a direct link westwards, via a linear pond and lawns, to the leisure pavilion. The pavilion is set into a hillock reached by a

MacCormac Jamieson Prichard 1993

MacCormac Jamieson Prichard 1993

swanky arched footbridge. A bar area opens out on to an outdoor terrace and pool beneath, both with views back towards the rest of the campus; a waterfall which gushes at a brisk staccato rate completes the vista. Also incorporated in the pavilion are a sports hall, gymnasium, dance studio, snooker room and squash court.

All materials used are of good quality and well detailed – grit-blasted concrete on exterior walls with bands of polished concrete blocks coloured with a green pigment. All steel work for balustrading, roof truss supports and curtain walling is powder-coated steel (raven grey). An unfathomable detail is the capital on all of the columns supporting the roofs and the colonnade in front of the accommodation block. It vaguely resembles a telephone jack. Inside, communal areas are defined by polished, hand-textured Italian plaster partition walls tinted a muted moss green, petrol blue and burnt red – all very tasteful.

The building as a whole has an ethereal quality, particularly from the outside – it is a modern stately home. Once inside the courtyard the atmosphere has the tranquility of a Japanese tea-garden but, sadly, the interior spaces lack this cohesion – cross-breeding corporate comfort (the company logo is acid-etched on to every glass classroom door) with working laboratory has resulted in up-market but conventional interiors.

STRUCTURAL ENGINEER Ove Arup & Partners
CONTRACT VALUE commisioned cost £14.3 million
GETTING THERE turning off the A45 near Canley marked by signs to main Warwick University campus and Westwood Business Park; go straight on round three roundabouts and the college is about a mile along Westwood Heath Road on the right-hand side
ACCESS very limited

West Midlands

MacCormac Jamieson Prichard 1993

MacCormac Jamieson Prichard 1993

J Sainsbury's Supermarket
Canley, Coventry

Coventry is a fascinating network of under- and over-passes, all tied up with a gyratory road system which leads you into the nowhere land of superstores and carpetworlds on the outskirts of town. Amongst the sprawl is a new Sainsbury's supermarket and petrol station, distinguished by their winged canopies glowing like UFOs in the darkness. I suggest you go at night to experience the full impact (and the traffic is not as bad so you can get away more quickly). During the day the effect is not quite as dramatic, especially in rain, when the flowing forms become flat and lost in the haze.

The architect's brief was to deal with the frontage of the supermarket and the canopy for the petrol station. The former is a 7-metre high by 65-metre-long Planar glass wall, interrupted by a protruding Portland-stone-clad block containing the newsagent and pharmacy, and all covered by the long canopy. The form and construction techniques employed are inspired by the Sopwith Pup light aircraft which were once manufactured on the site. Tubular supports are spanned by steel aerofoil frames across the top with an opaque PVC-coated polyester fabric stretched cover. On the underside is a PVC-coated polyester mesh which, when illuminated at night, reveals the profiles of the frames inside. Various types of halide projector have been used to define a zone of light along the frontage. At the petrol station, a much more bulbous form, projectors define light zones over the pumps. Zumtobel uplighters fill the rest of the outdoor spaces with light.

The canopy provides shelter for the trolleys, the 'pick-up point', cash machines and some bizarrely located bench seating looking out towards the car park. Customers still get drenched while battling through the rain from canopy to car.

Lifschutz Davidson 1994

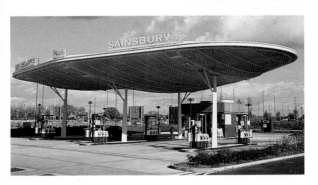

West Midlands

Lifschutz Davidson 1994

The supermarket itself is exactly the same as any other in the country. The front elevation to the supermarket and the mushroom-shaped canopy at the petrol station are interventions acting as beacons in a blank landscape. The architect has not been asked to readdress the grocery-shopping experience but to make the supermarket stand out without resorting to exaggerated graphics or fairground-lighting tactics.

This Sainsbury's store is one of a series of new regional supermarkets designed by a series of architects who have an eye for more than the pastoral pastiche so often found in superstore developments. Look out for those in Plymouth by Dixon . Jones (page 254) and in Harlow, Essex by Terry Farrell (page 196).

West Midlands

STRUCTURAL ENGINEER Ernest Green Partnership/Buro Happold
CLIENT J Sainsbury plc
SIZE 6000 square metres
GETTING THERE located on Tile Hill Lane, Canley, part of the A45 going towards Birmingham
ACCESS open

Lifschutz Davidson 1994

West Midlands

Lifschutz Davidson 1994

Nelson Mandela Community Primary School

Sparkbrook, Birmingham

This building received RIBA's Building of the Year Award in 1989, nominated by the then President of the RIBA, Maxwell Hutchinson. The award signified the rift that exists between 'architects' architecture' and an architecture for everyone else. The building is not dazzling technologically or stylistically; by choosing it Hutchinson focused the conversation on the importance of building according to the needs of the type and its occupants: in this case, children, teachers and parents. His award speech described it as: 'a school designed totally around the needs of the children and the community. This building is not full of no-go areas. It is concerned with what children can do rather than what they cannot do'.

The school is located in the centre of Birmingham in a residential area with a large immigrant population, primarily Punjabi. For 93 per cent of the pupils English is a second language, so an interpreter is assigned to each class. The inspiration for the layout of the building came from the work of the Hampshire County Architects Department with their tradition of single-storey pitched-roof buildings focusing on an internal 'street' and a more open-plan classroom layout.

The Nelson Mandela School is a long low shed. Its corrugated pitched roof has a generous overhang at the sides forming promenades on the north and south elevations. A central street runs down the middle of the building; teaching and ancillary spaces line each side of it. The classrooms are laid out in a repetitive pattern: two classes with an adjoining craft room on the south opening out on to the playground, and quiet reading rooms on the north. The classrooms are divided by sliding partitions so there is the opportunity for classes to merge for some activities.

The street is also used as a teaching area and provides a place for chil-

West Midlands

W G Reed, Birmingham City Architect 1987

W G Reed, Birmingham City Architect 1987

dren to sit and work alone or in a group. The layout promotes collaborative teaching and learning and the open access means that pupils and teachers mingle. Halfway along the shed on the north side is the main entrance, with the main hall opposite on the south. The street is bright and airy, top-lit by rooflights, and the structure is soft: a timber frame with exposed laminated timber trusses. Walls between classrooms are glazed above head height to allow light to filter uninterrupted all the way along the ceiling, reducing the need for artificial lighting. I visited the building on what must have been the gloomiest and rainiest day of the year but lights were not needed in the central street area.

The nursery pupils at the far west semi-detached end of the building get a harsh deal, forced to play outside on the rough concrete and penned in with barriers to keep them under shelter but away from the rain-sodden playground. Despite this and the mandatory primary colours assigned to steelwork and exterior timber roof trusses, the spaces seem to work well and the teachers confirm that they enjoy working there because 'everything has been thought about – down to the soft rubber inner-tube edging on sliding doors so small fingers don't get squashed'.

STRUCTURAL ENGINEER Birmingham City Engineer
CLIENT Birmingham City Council Education and Leisure Services Committee
SIZE: 2370 square metres
CONTRACT VALUE £1.8 million
GETTING THERE go to the Birmingham inner ring road, follow signs to Sparkhill, then Sparkbrook
ACCESS announce yourself to the headteacher at reception before wandering around

West Midlands

W G Reed, Birmingham City Architect 1987

West Midlands

W G Reed, Birmingham City Architect 1987

International Convention Centre
Birmingham

The International Convention Centre is the UK's largest. It includes a first-class Symphony Hall (home of the Birmingham Philharmonic Orchestra), 11 halls, a mall, restaurants and a new public square. The whole complex (and the 16-hectare site) is a major coherent intervention into a city well known for its urban chaos. The National Exhibition Centre, built 20 years ago on the outskirts of Birmingham, has proved to be a major asset, attracting people from all over the world. The Convention Centre will draw visitors further into the city centre, filling the new Hyatt Hotel and providing performing-arts facilities for the local population.

The architects carried out a townscape study looking at ways of linking the city centre with the new site. It revealed five key issues: buildings had to be massed to avoid dominating the surroundings; pedestrian access from the city centre across the inner ring road had to be provided without building a bridge or digging an underpass; a major new public space had to be provided (the solution was to create the 10,000-square-metre Centenary Square, designed by artist Tess Jaray); a mall linking all the halls and providing a direct route from Centenary Square through to Canal Side, to include restaurant and banking facilities was needed; the siting of a 2200-seat Symphony Hall when there is a railway running underneath.

Artec Consultants Inc from New York worked closely with the architects, producing more than 70 models in order to achieve the excellent acoustics that the concert hall now boasts. The traditional rectangular form encourages a strong lateral sound which gives listeners the impression of surround sound. Three modern devices help to vary that environment: openable reverberation chambers (a series of volumes behind the platform connected by doors which can be opened or closed to alter

Convention Centre Partnership 1983–91

the 'livenesss' of the hall), acoustic curtains (sliding screens made of absorbent materials on all the interior walls), and an acoustic canopy (a sound reflector located above the platform which can be set at different levels according to the scale of the performance – it also houses additional lighting and speakers). Rubber mountings on voided piles and structural isolation joints obliterate noise and vibration from the rail tunnel below. The Symphony organ, made in Germany, forms the backdrop to the platform. Interior finishes are granite and hardwood, with deep salmon-pink upholstery and columns creating a comfortable, warm atmosphere.

The concert hall is undoubtedly the highlight of this whole complex. The architects have been successful in massing the buildings so that they do not blunder into their surroundings. Elevations are windowless (except for the abstract glacial wall facing Centenary Square) and therefore anonymous stone-clad walls. Although the mass of building is vast it goes by almost unnoticed. The focus is definitely on an interior environment, and Centenary Square with its patterned brick carpet has become the external feature for the buildings.

ASSOCIATED ARCHITECTS Percy Thomas Partnership and Renton Howard Wood Levin Partnership
STRUCTURAL ENGINEER Ove Arup & Partners
CLIENT City of Birmingham
SIZE Symphony Hall seats 2200, Conference Hall seats 1500, Centenary Square is 10,000 square metres
GETTING THERE follow signs from the inner ring road
ACCESS open

West Midlands

Convention Centre Partnership 1983–91

Broadfield House Glass Museum – Glass Pavilion
Kingswinford

The Glass Pavilion was built as a part of a plan to create a new entrance, reception area and museum shop at the rear of the original building. It also happens to be at the cutting edge of architectural glass innovation, and is believed to be the largest glass structure of its kind in the world.

Architects and engineers collaborated closely to create an entirely glass building with no metal supports or connectors (with the exception of the rendered blockwork gable end). Beams and columns are made from three sheets of plate glass laminated together to form structural frames and jointed using a glass mortice and tenon. Roof construction is particularly interesting, the panels designed to create a satisfactory working climate inside the pavilion and to moderate heat and coolness. The outer layer is 10 mm Cool-Lite K Neutral, a specially coated glass manufactured in Holland. A microscopic layer of silver is laid on the inner surface to inhibit solar gain; the effect is virtually transparent, unlike tinted or reflective glass. The inner layer is made up of two sheets of toughened glass laminated together. The inner face has a pattern of ceramic frit coating on the surface to act as a solar reflector and integral blind over the reception area. There is a 10 mm air cavity in between for insulation. The walls are made of 8 mm glass, admitting 61 per cent of natural light into the museum.

Dudley Council aims to develop Himley Hall, formerly the home of the Earls of Dudley as the new national glass museum. This project, a showcase for the development, is small but its achievement is tremendous.

STRUCTURAL ENGINEER Dewhurst MacFarlane & Partners
GETTING THERE Compton Drive
ACCESS open

West Midlands

West Midlands

Design Antenna 1994

School of Engineering and Manufacturing, De Montfort University
Leicester

What has this project not got? Every continent seems to be represented in the aesthetic make-up of this set of buildings: Gothic revival, Swiss chalet, New England beach house, Moorish palace, Victorian industrial. However, the more interesting proposition for the buildings is based on the idea that large buildings can be ventilated naturally. The architects tried an integrated approach to minimising energy use by using the form and fabric to moderate the internal environment. The buildings are designed to cope with double the amount of heat gain generated by a dealing room in the City.

Spaces are shallow, orientated for maximum light and insulation with cross and stack-effect ventilation to remove heat. An example of this can be seen most easily in one of the two auditoria. At the back of the room there is an opening – you find yourself at the base of a quilted shaft, rather like being at the bottom of a manhole in the road. This is a ventilation tower, drawing up warm air and expelling it through a vent in the top.

The internal organisation is focused around a 50-metre central spine which extends to full-height, flanked on the north side by the auditoria and on the south side by the double-height General Laboratory.

The main eastern entrance is via a courtyard surrounded on two sides by the Electrical Laboratories. The west wing is occupied by the Mechanical Laboratories. The interior of the spine is a sight to behold – a dense arrangement of thick, round steel columns supporting a semi-translucent walkway above, with decorative dagger-like projections thrusting into the dark space below. A few minute stand-up coffee-bar tables are clustered around one column – a hanging-out area perhaps? This space has been created for 'random interaction' – apparently the school is

Leicestershire

Short Ford and Associates 1993

Leicestershire

Short Ford and Associates 1993

committed to the integration of all levels of engineering and research. Everywhere you look you are surrounded by peppermint green walls and heavy steelwork. Stuffy corridors link to other wings, with the carpet-tiled cafeteria is stuffed down at the western end. Steel-grilled steps (creating a prison clatter) lead you through the central space to upper floors with views through windows into the General Laboratory.

The top floor houses the design studios. Ranks of drawing boards are set up in a formal curve and banks of computer terminals snake away in the opposite direction leaving blank unused spaces in between. The most grating detail of all is the thick plastic electrical ducting which runs from each terminal around the room, getting thicker and thicker as it collects more threads, stamping out other interior surfaces and detailing in its path, like an unpleasant growth.

The project's style was drawn from the Puginesque notion that the Middle Ages provided a model of both logical design and beautiful building – 'plan follows programme'. Whether this has been interpreted entirely successfully here is debatable. The catalogue of decorative elements and materials (from red brick with red mortar to cedar shingle) that covers the whole building might have proven to be more truthful to the plan if they had not been detailed so shabbily.

STRUCTURAL ENGINEER YRM Anthony Hunt Associates
CLIENT De Montfort University
SIZE 10,000 square metres
CONTRACT VALUE £8.5 million
GETTING THERE The Queen's Building, The Gateway, Leicester
ACCESS announce yourself at reception. It is easier to get in during term

Leicestershire

Short Ford and Associates 1993

Leicestershire

Inland Revenue Headquarters
Nottingham

This project is speculative in the sense that Bracken House in London, also by Michael Hopkins & Partners, was speculative – designed for the needs of one client but with the possibility that they might want to inhabit a part of the site and lease out other areas or, alternatively, gradually expand themselves. Initially, 2000 employees will be moving in.

The offices are in six large buildings. Two are planned around a quadrangle and four are L-shaped in plan. The focus of the site on the north side is the Teflon-coated glassfibre fabric-roofed Amenities Building. The massing of the buildings and their interconnecting avenues all radiate from the notional nucleus of the site – the castle on the hill. Four-storey blocks are sited nearer the hill, with three-storey blocks sloping away on the south side. In between there will be avenues of trees and car-parking spaces delineated by granite setts. A contrast is created between inside and outside, buildings are not linked together with covered walkways. This is a familiar Hopkins trait (see Schlumberger Research, page 44); shelter is provided by a generous supply of umbrellas at every doorway.

Each element in the project can be linked to a previous Hopkins building: brick piers supporting shallow arches from Glyndebourne, shallow balconies and sliding windows from Solid State Logic and Schlumberger; glass brick and red brick from the Lord's Mound Stand; ceiling construction from the David Mellor Factory and Glyndebourne; slim pre-cast concrete lintels from Bracken House and Glyndebourne. and fabric roof structure from Schlumberger and the Buckingham Palace ticket booth. Lessons have been learned from these buildings and elements have been adapted to suit the quick-build nature of this project. There are also developments in creating an entirely passively ventilated building. The blocks, in almost every respect, are prefabricated, except

Michael Hopkins & Partners 1995

Michael Hopkins & Partners 1995

for the ground-floor slabs and service cores which were cast in-situ. The corner towers were made in round storey-high sections and slotted on top of each other, and the solid brick piers were brought in ready made as a time-saving measure, whereas at Glyndebourne the walls were laid brick by brick. The two construction methods are appropriate to their individual buildings and the clients' requirements.

Internally, the rippling ceiling panels were pre-cast, accommodating light- and speaker-fittings, with a shape that directs natural light on to the rows of desks while trapping heat in the soffits. The 3.2- metre-wide by 13.6-metre-deep structural bays are open-plan but the internal desk arrangements are again determined by the pattern of ceiling panels. Full-height windows open onto shallow balconies. A stack effect is created in the corner towers – the tower roof lifts open by a metre, raised by a jack suspended by spoke ties to the top of each tower, a piece of machinery specially developed for this project. You can get a good view of this operation from the generous helical stairs inside the towers, but sadly not from the outside which is shrouded in thick glass brick.

The tower roofs are controlled by a weather station on Building E which indicates whether the tower roof should be up or down. Another system resets the window blinds at lunchtime and at 5pm; in between, employees can direct them as they please. The attention to detail in these areas was achieved by the blending of budgets – economies were found in other areas in the building for the sake of perfecting these aspects of the construction. The top-floor levels, as in another of Hopkins' schemes, are cantilevered to increase floor space and reduce the sheer verticality of the exterior elevations. Pitched roofs lined in plywood and supported by steel trusses and purlins create potentially bright loft spaces, but the windows are so low beneath the eaves that views out are of the walls of

Nottinghamshire

Michael Hopkins & Partners 1995

Michael Hopkins & Partners 1995

neighbouring buildings rather than sky.

The Amenities Building is a recreational block. It includes a sports hall at the centre in a lofty double-height space directly beneath the fabric roof, flanked by two wings accommodating on the ground floor changing rooms, the kitchen, and a nursery, with a restaurant and bar on the first-floor. Where the membrane roof meets the side wings, eye-shaped windows fill the gaps so that the single piece of fabric seems to float independently above the wings. Both north and south ends are clear glazed but unfortunately the edge of the fabric stretches down too far, cutting off a view of the castle up the hill.

The office buildings have a Victorian warehouse aesthetic and proportiona inside and out, like the nearby canal warehouses. Shallow arches, heavy brick piers, dark metal windows, the shallow relief of the external elevations and low ceiling heights inside contribute to the atmosphere. The repetition of structural elements and motifs, even though they are refined or altered a little in each project, is wearing thin. Hopkins had a tremendous sensitivity towards materials in earlier projects where he primarily used steel and glass, but since the move towards brick and concrete and an attempt to handle them as prefabricated materials, the results have undeniably been more conservative.

STRUCTURAL ENGINEER Ove Arup & Partners
SIZE 40,000 square metres
CONTRACT VALUE £50 million
GETTING THERE on the edge of Nottingham Canal, access from Wilford Street
ACCESS very limited

Nottinghamshire

Michael Hopkins & Partners 1995

Nottinghamshire

Michael Hopkins & Partners 1995

Cambridgeshire and Bedfordshire

Schlumberger Research Ltd
Cambridge

Schlumberger Cambridge Research is a multi-national group providing technical services to oil-exploration companies. Its UK arm investigates drilling and fluid mechanics, rock and well-bore physics and the computer modelling of drilling information. The company needed a new research facility and a test station to house a simulated drilling rig, requiring a clear height inside of 10 metres. Schlumberger is a patron of good design – its other main research facility in Connecticut was designed by Philip Johnson, and their Paris headquarters by Renzo Piano. Hopkins was chosen to add to this prestigious list because his proposal was courageous and experimental, like the client's work.

Sited on high ground just outside Cambridge on land belonging to the University, the project has been built in two phases. The tented structure was built first and is the focus as a prototype construction. The main entrance building on the south side was added seven years later, borrowing from earlier Hopkins projects, particularly the Solid State Logic building in Oxfordshire (see page 352). The phase 1 brief stressed the importance of maximum contact between departments: research and computing labs, manufacturing services and offices share a similar quality and flexibility of environment. The solution was to put the test station at the heart of the building and surround it with offices and recreational areas for the other departments so that they could all have the same clear view of the focus of the company's interest. The resulting design puts offices (looking out through full-height sliding windows) and laboratories (looking in through a glazed wall) in two single-storey strips on the east and west sides of the north-facing test station (formed from two 24 x 18-metre bays) and the south-facing winter garden, which contains a full-height restaurant and library (formed from a third 24 x 18-metre bay).

Michael Hopkins & Partners 1985 and 1992

Cambridgeshire

Michael Hopkins & Partners 1985 and 1992

The roof membrane is structurally independent of the office wings and is made of Teflon-coated glassfibre fabric with a life expectancy of 30 years (at the time of construction it was the biggest installation of this kind in the country). It is supported by trusses which span 24 metres and 50-mm solid tension rods which are in turn supported by hollow-section struts. A second rod can take the load if one fails.

The offices wings are based on Hopkins' Patera prefabricated package building system. Apart from the concrete ground slab, no wet trades are involved and all the components are made from inorganic materials. Each 18-metre-long wing is a flat-roofed box with an external trussed structure (here the sides are supported by single columns as opposed to the trussed sides of the original Patera design) supporting glass and insulated steel cladding panels, coated in zinc-metal spray. Inside, the offices and meeting spaces have an internal cladding system made of a draw-on-and-wipe-off surface so there are diagrams and sketches all over the walls. Behind this type of building is the idea that the simplicity of parts and minimalist detailing create unity in the design, shown by the integration of the two systems – the tent and the box wings. A complex service network run through the floors meant that layers of chipboard were sandwiched within the floor to provide access – not part of the original streamlined Patera design.

One or two aspects of the building have been less successful and have been changed. The winter garden has needed additional heating (warm-air heating was used instead of the underfloor system proposed in the original concept). Access, which was originally to one side of the south-facing elevation, has been centred to bring it into line with the new entrance in the phase 2 building.

There is a vista from the south-facing entrance of the latest building,

Michael Hopkins & Partners 1985 and 1992

Michael Hopkins & Partners 1985 and 1992

via the reception inside a central two-storey atrium, out the other side, across an open courtyard and up some steps to the phase 1 building. This transition, going outside from one building to another, is a familiar Hopkins theme, always accompanied by large umbrella stands at each door (see Inland Revenue, page 250). Here, the courtyard is not actually bounded by walls but suggested as a route by the definition of an edge between the paving and the surrounding lawns, and the southward protrusion of the office wings of the phase 1 building flanking the steps.

The phase 2 building is made up of two wings either side of the central double-height atrium space, which forms a bridge. The wings are square in plan and externally very much like the Solid State Logic building. Here the floors are divided up into perimeter cellular offices. There is one diagonal staircase extending from the east and west sides (two each side at Solid State) – proportions are altogether smaller and closer to the ground with slightly more ornate pre-cast concrete eaves cantilevering the second-floor level.

There is a spirit to these buildings that is similar to Foster's Renault Distribution Centre in Swindon – an innovative thoroughness which makes the project stand out. The whole concept has been addressed – from the design of the restaurant tables to the unique roof structure – to encompass the diverse requirements of a company in a variety of spaces.

STRUCTURAL ENGINEER Anthony Hunt Associates
MEMBRANE AND CABLE ENGINEERING Ove Arup & Partners
GETTING THERE exit junction 13 off the M11, turn left at the lights and take the second turning on the left again, signposted to High Cross Research Park – you will see the roof from here
ACCESS very limited and strictly by prior arrangement … if you are lucky

Cambridgeshire

Michael Hopkins & Partners 1985 and 1992

Michael Hopkins & Partners 1985 and 1992

Fitzwilliam College Chapel
Cambridge

The chapel punctuates the end of a wall of student housing designed by Denys Lasdun in the 1960s. A timber core rises out of a brick skin. Entering through the heavy but very smooth timber door at ground level, you are led around the edge of the building by a gently curving stairway up into the main chapel. There is nothing overtly religious in the way that the elements of the chapel have been detailed: instead of stained glass a large east-facing clear window behind the altar pushes outwards through the brick envelope. The glass is divided by steel glazing bars and looks on to a grand old tree. There are no tapestry prayer cushions, no ostentatious flower arrangements, no put-the-fear-of-God-into-you collages.

The purity of the atmosphere is enhanced by the softness of the light wood interior and the way that natural light falls through the glass slots on each side of the altar, hitting the shallow domed ceiling over the organ, and from above through a timber clerestory, throwing curves of light down the side walls.

STRUCTURAL ENGINEER Ove Arup & Partners
CLIENT Fitzwilliam College, Cambridge
SIZE 350 square metres
CONTRACT VALUE £500,000
GETTING THERE on the Huntingdon Road, A1307 north out of Cambridge city centre
ACCESS announce your presence at the college before you wander around

Cambridgeshire

MacCormac Jamieson Prichard 1991

Cambridgeshire

MacCormac Jamieson Prichard 1991

St John's College Library
Cambridge

The front entrance to the library is located in Chapel Court, one of three courts that make up the college, standing opposite Gilbert Scott's neo-Gothic chapel and next to Edward Maufe's student residences (called sets) which were built in in the 1930s. The library itself penetrates the Penrose building (1885) on the south-west corner of the court. The original building had been adapted so many times that its original internal arrangement was no longer coherent. Cullinan chose to convert the building yet again but this time by adding a new axis to the original plan, thus providing more accommodation and creating a new entrance.

The new wing pentrates right through the Penrose building and out the other side into the Master's garden. This axis is an elongated version of the formal entrance to the old building that already existed a few metres to the right of the new library, on the same west side of the court, even down to the lantern and apsidal west-facing end. The exterior detailing is bland and crude, drawing in a modified form of window tracery from the neo-Gothic chapel and the pitch of the Penrose building roof – the aping and collaging of already mediocre styles is plainly bad-form.

Internally the new addition is more successful. A climate-control system was developed by Max Fordham Associates. When it is cold, warm air is drawn by convection from workspaces and bookstacks into a central duct at the intersection between new and old wings marked by a lift shaft surrounded by a spiral staircase, then drawn up to the lantern at the top. The air is then pushed back down by a punka fan inside the base of the spire and escapes through window frames and slots in the walls. When it is hot, a flap rises automatically inside the spire and warm air is expelled through the top.

The double-height space of the old lecture rooms has been maintained,

Cambridgeshire

Edward Cullinan Architects 1993

Cambridgeshire

Edward Cullinan Architects 1993

the issue desk on the ground floor and a mezzanine inserted to accommodate reading desks along one edge looking inwards on the first floor level. The main area of inhabitation is the apsidal end with offices on the ground floor and reading desks (some with views out on to the Master's garden) and bookstacks on the first floor. The amount of space allocated for reading and books is relatively very small and a large proportion of the space is given over to circulation.

It has been said that much insight into an architect's work can be derived from the style and quality of his or her shoes. If the work itself were to be compared to a pair of shoes then this building would be a pair of Hush Puppies, the type commonly worn by traffic wardens.

Cambridgeshire

STRUCTURAL ENGINEER Hammah Reed & Associates
CLIENT St John's College
GETTING THERE St John's Street, Cambridge
ACCESS limited

Edward Cullinan Architects 1993

Rare Books Repository, Newnham College
Cambridge

This stocky brick and lead-lidded treasure-chest houses the rare book collection from Newnham College Library in a suitably climate-controlled and secure environment. The architects wanted to adopt some of the qualities of Basil Champneys' original library building (1896). This was achieved by tracing the dimensions of its central nave on to the section of the repository and by adopting the barrel-vaulted ceiling and the 19th-century notion of a mezzanine level.

The building's monolithic quality was determined by the strict brief that it had to be secure against fire and theft, and a stable temperature had to be maintained. Natural convection currents on wall surfaces are encouraged by underfloor heating and extractor fans in the rooflight, providing the right conditions for conservation of the book bindings (the books stand 150 mm away from the wall to allow air movement). A rooflight running the length of the building provides indirect natural light but levels have to be low so cheap additional lighting has been added. A very tight budget has determined the choice of steel furniture and mezzanine which have all been made up from standard steel units and painted grey.

With its solitary reading table on the ground floor, the interior oozes the intimacy of a secret garret, the stuff of which I am sure many prospective Cambridge students dream.

STRUCTURAL ENGINEER Fogg Associates
CLIENT Peter Insk, bursar, Newnham College
SIZE 94 square metres
GETTING THERE Sidgwick Avenue, Cambridge
ACCESS very limited

Cambridgeshire

Joanna van Heyningen and Birkin Haward Architects 1982

Joanna van Heyningen and Birkin Haward Architects 1982

Post-graduate Study Centre, Darwin College
Cambridge

From Silver Street the study centre is no more than a 45-metre-long lime-mortar wall, gently curved to follow the line of the pavement (soft lime mortar is used to avoid movement joints). From the south-east-facing River Cam side, a simple fenestrated timber deck leans out over a brick base, like a houseboat with cantilevered supports as oars. As the wall suggests, and as is emphasised by the shallow clerestory window running its full length, the plan is a long, thin corridor continuing the chain of college buildings that line the street.

The study centre is more than just a library in that it accommodates books and computers, a seminar room and a flat. The architects have provided different kinds of working environments to respond to the variety of facilities and study moods of the students. Entrance is via a double-height reading room with a large picture-window view on to the Cam. The plan is then split into three lengthways along the building. On the north-west side, a book-lined arterial corridor at ground-floor level with three staircases leads up to a long, south-east-facing built-in reading bench from which you can gaze at the passing river traffic. The central strip has now been cut into four sections by the book-lined staircases, so on the ground floor they form enclosed computer rooms and U-shaped reading platforms upstairs. Seating (chrome mesh and black leather) is by Eames. The roof is lifted on both sides by strips of windows flooding the space with natural light. External cantilevered balconies provide yet another atmosphere in which to study.

The entire building is dominated by the unseasoned timber construction. The interior has been conceived as one piece of furniture: structure (post-and-beam frame and rafters), cladding, windows, floors, bookcases

Jeremy Dixon . Edward Jones 1994

Jeremy Dixon . Edward Jones 1994

and furniture are made of unseasoned English oak. To avoid opening windows on the street side, a timber lantern is located at the apex of the plan. This opens and closes automatically to provide cross-ventilation to the reading room.

The architects have used this awkwardly shaped site to their advantage and have invented an understated building without adopting or aping traditional building forms. There is precision in the detailing where different materials meet, and a satisfying robustness in the timber construction.

Cambridgeshire

STRUCTURAL ENGINEER Ove Arup & Partners
CLIENT Darwin College
SIZE 750 square metres
CONTRACT VALUE £1 million
GETTING THERE Silver Street, Cambridge
ACCESS very limited (closed during holiday periods)

Cambridgeshire

Jeremy Dixon . Edward Jones 1994

The Howard Building, Downing College
Cambridge

Gavin Stamp was politically correct in giving Quinlan Terry the benefit of the doubt in his critique of the Howard Building in the 16 March 1988 issue of *The Architects' Journal*: 'This building is … either praised or condemned solely because of the employment of a classical style. What has not been asked is what matters about a building in any style: does it succeed in its own terms? Is it any good as architecture?' A brief look at the jumble of quasi-classical details soon reveals that it is no more than a staid, pompous, inarticulate and crude display of a fragmented understanding of the Palladian ethos – academic one-liners. Quoting again from Stamp: 'Palladio wrote, "Beauty will result from the form and correspondence of the whole, with respect to the several parts with regard to each other and of these again to the whole; that the structure may appear an entire and complete body, wherein each member agrees with the other, and all necessary to compose what you intend to form".' The last phrase seems to be particularly apt in this case … but judge for yourself.

See for yourself the collection of details strewn across the façades of this two-storey building (its main purpose is to house a lecture hall, situated on the first floor). The north façade has been adorned to shout 'main entrance'; the central bay emphasised by a pediment on Corinthian columns and doors surmounted by a mannerist flourish, curvaceous pediment and coat-of-arms. The doors are locked. Side doors and french windows on the south side are more commonly used to access the ground-floor foyer. The south façade displays a balustraded balcony supported by baseless Doric columns. Square, fluted Corinthian columns define each corner of the building, like a wedding cake. There is absolutely no relationship between the front, back and end elevations and the interior spaces. The exterior is a catalogue of pastiche details and the interior

Erith & Terry Architects 1987

Erith & Terry Architects 1987

compiled of an arbitrary arrangement of rooms which have no connection with their envelope.

On a campus with buildings designed by William Wilkins (chapel, 1805), E M Barry (west end of the campus, 1873) and Sir Herbert Baker (Kenny Court), all faithfully executed in the Greek revival style, the least Terry could have done was to adopt the same plinth level. The architect and I agree on one thing: neither of us is a member of the blending-in school of architecture. This is no more classical revival than the Observer Building in London.

The building was endowed by the Howard Trust, established by Dr Alan Howard, inventor of the Cambridge Diet. Perhaps the trustees could be a little more abstemious when they choose an architect for future college projects.

Cambridgeshire

STRUCTURAL ENGINEER Pennington and Partners
CLIENT Downing College
SIZE 495 square metres
CONTRACT VALUE £1,015,101
GETTING THERE Tennis Court Road, Cambridge
ACCESS limited

Erith & Terry Architects 1987

Cambridgeshire

Erith & Terry Architects 1987

Cambridge Crystallographic Data Centre

This building is the result of an exceptional client/architect relationship. The Danish architect Erik Sorensen was first recommended to Olga Kennard by the eminent physicist Nils Bohr at Copenhagen Univeristy, in the 1950s. Sorensen proceeded to build a family house for Kennard in 1959.

The Cambridge Crystallographic Data Centre compiles a computer database containing comprehensive information for organic and organo-metallic compounds studied by x-ray and neutron diffraction methods. The database is used in the pharmacological and chemical industries which provide the financial support for the centre's charitable status.

The whole building has been designed in response to the specific requirements of the centre, set out by the client without trying to influence the way that the building might look in the end. One particular require-ment was that the light in working areas be subdued because of the use of computer screens by all the staff. This rule goes against all the ideals of making glorious, light-filled working environments where employees can be in touch with their surroundings and benefit from natural light. Here, the architect has ingeniously combined a south-facing atrium (protruding out of the top of the building like a huge curved air-duct) with deep mezzanine floors, carving out an interior space with natural and localised areas of light and soft materials rather than subdividing it with partitions and harsh universal artificial lighting. The centre of the atrium is pierced by a glass-sided lift. Walls are fair-faced acoustic blockwork and ceilings lined in dark hardwood, the softness of both materials creating a monastic hush throughout the building. There is an inglenook fireplace located on the first floor refering to a cosy domestic environment rather than trying to enforce an institutional atmosphere.

Cambridgeshire

Erik Sorensen (Zibranettsen Architects) 1992

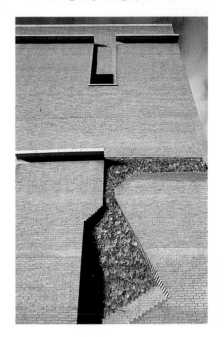

Cambridgeshire

Erik Sorensen (Zibranettsen Architects) 1992

Many of the materials and components used were also made in Denmark. Bricks, perforated blockwork, Dutch carpets supplied and laid by a Danish firm, and a Danish smith made all the window frames, partition frames, and furniture legs and lamps (all fittings were designed by Sorensen). Other distinctive furniture specified for the centre includes lunch room chairs by Paul Kjaerholm, cutlery by Georg Jensen, china is Royal Copenhagen blue and renovated Eames chairs at work stations.

The external façade is unlikely in its austerity, thin layers of sheer red-brick, punctured by small window openings and punctuated by broken cornices, drawn like dotted lines across the front. The layers of brick have been spliced away around window openings and on the right-hand side of the entrance door, grafted away to reveal a crystal seam. Embedded in the entrance hall floor is an glass-encased octagonal pool containing growing crystals which can also be viewed from underneath from the basement floor. These direct references to the focus of activitiy within the building should not be misconstrued as sentimental decorations but are integral to the make-up of the building as a total environment where every detail has been addressed and expressed humanely.

Cambridgeshire

STRUCTURAL ENGINEER W S Atkins
CLIENT Olga Kennard (Scientific Director of the Cambridge Crystallographic Data Centre)
GETTTING THERE Union Road is in the Newtown area, south of the city; the centre backs onto the university chemistry building
ACCESS limited

Erik Sorensen (Zibranettsen Architects) 1992

Ellis-Miller House
Prickwillow

The single-storey, steel-framed house is on the west edge of Prickwillow, a working agricultural village, with views over the Cambridgeshire Fens and Ely Cathedral. The architect's intention was to take advantage of the stunning view and its vast skies while trying to create an architecture that would rest easily in an unforgiving landscape on a very slim budget.

The plan of the house is three bays long, two enclosed and the third covered but open-sided to form a large porch area. The enclosed bays are then divided longitudinally with the study/sitting room space on the west side facing the Fens, lined by full-height, double-glazed windows. Externally this face is shrouded in full-height external Venetian blinds which obscure views into the house from the road to the west side of the house and provide protection from excessive heat gain during the summer. Internally this is an open-plan space with only the subtlest of partitioning in the form of a free-standing fireplace and flue. The east side accommodates a bedroom, a bathroom and kitchen and is clad on the outside with profiled metal sheeting punctuated by a thin horizonatal line of windows.

There is a history of modern single-storey houses set in semi-rural locations, such as the Farnsworth House by Mies van der Rohe and the Johnson House by Philip Johnson (both in the USA). Both these projects are set in substantial private grounds maximising the best views by making the walls out of glass. Both houses hover above ground on short legs and the glass walls are fully exposed with services in the centre of the plan, leaving the perimeter free as communal space. The Ellis-Miller house differs in that neighbouring buildings are close by, so it crouches close to the ground, nestling in shrubbery. Its façades are obscured in various ways to maintain some privacy from passers-by, and the entire internal volume is divided in such a way that all living activities are allo-

Cambridgeshire

Jonathan Ellis-Miller Architects 1993

Cambridgeshire

Jonathan Ellis-Miller Architects 1993

cated to specific areas. The plan encompasses the external environment by covering the terrace area.

Unfortunately, detailing is neither as imaginative nor as thorough as that of Mies or Johnson – skirting boards are fussy and doors are set into the walls with frames, details which would have been more in keeping with the prefabricated/machine-made ideal if they had been flush surfaces as in the treatment of the exterior walls. All the houses share a simplicity of form, minimalisation of servicing facilities, and desire to embrace their surroundings and, of course, the Ellis-Miller house is a triumph over conventional rural planning.

Cambridgeshire

CLIENT Jonathan Ellis-Miller
GETING THERE Prickwillow, Cambridgeshire
ACCESS very limited

Jonathan Ellis-Miller Architects 1993

Cambridgeshire

Jonathan Ellis-Miller Architects 1993

Library, Cranfield University

Lying low in the Bedfordshire landscape is a collection of undistinguished aircraft hangars, laboratories and teaching bunkers making up the distinguished Cranfield University campus – Britain's top education and research establishment for advanced technology, solely for post-graduate students. The buildings were once part of a World War 2 Royal Air Force training school; the adjacent airfield is still in use.

The library was commissioned because a new focus was needed for the campus and information technology was rapidly becoming a facility that needed to be available to each student. John Bladgen, head librarian, researched the library model, looking at examples of the building type all over the world, but found nothing that expressed what he felt was important in such a building. He was looking for a light-filled, transparent building conducive to study instead of the traditional dark space with endless rows of dust-covered volumes and students hunched over tables in order to get close to dim desk lamps.

The outcome is thoroughly beautiful. The perfectly square plan is in two layers: a three-storey glass box shrouded by a barrel-vaulted canopy on tall slender columns with a veil of external blinds on the east and west sides. The roof, four bays wide, projects beyond the south-facing glazed frontage to form a covered forecourt. The glazed walls on the sides are set back from the edge of the roof line with the large, external louvres on the top two floors fixed between flat tapering columns, forming a covered colonnade on each side of the building.

A wide revolving glass door set to the right of centre leads you into an atriumed entrance foyer, a polished stone floor, and a 13-metre-long stainless-steel bar table on your right (for students and tutors to meet at and drink coffee), glass-tread stairs on the left. Atriums draw the eye up, but here it draws your eye up and forwards because the stairs stretch out

Sir Norman Foster & Partners 1993

Bedfordshire

Bedfordshire

Sir Norman Foster & Partners 1993

directly in front of you, tapering between first and second floors, and the rooflights draw a line towards the large window at the far end on the second floor. The ground floor accommodates seminar rooms and a lecture hall, all situated on the perimeter of the building.

The first and second floors are open plan, surrounding the atrium and linked by a bridge across the south end. There is a continuous workbench all the way around the front and sides of these two floors, designed by Norman and Sabhia Foster to accommodate individual students' personal computers and library information-technology stations. Relatively few books are stored in the open stacks because so much of the material is on computer and easily accessed. The desk faces outwards with views of the airfield on the east, the car park on the south, and trees on the west. There is plenty of natural light all the way around and continuous views across the internal space through bookstack avenues and between the books themselves. Subtle artificial lighting is reflected from the barrel-vaulted ceilings.

Each bay has a glazed rooflight running the full depth of the building, beneath which are standard strip lights shielded by a 'seagull-wing' shade (also running the full depth) made of perforated white steel sheet. This throws the even white light into the barrels.

The devices which define the interior space and the detailing go hand in hand. The choice of materials throughout is perfect, always simple and well-defined. The edges where one material meets another are always impeccable, such as the underside of the smooth concrete floorslabs meeting the steel-angle bannister railings, the stainless-steel door surrounds, and on the ground floor where a thin black line of skirting tiling (the same depth as the glass stair treads) meets the fair-faced blockwork walls.

Bedfordshire

Sir Norman Foster & Partners 1993

Sir Norman Foster & Partners 1993

Meticulous and painstaking, the entire building emerges out of the context of the site without being literal or authoritarian. It remains within the scale of the surrounding structures but just manages to float a metre or so above the sheds and hangars as if preparing for lift-off. This is well worth visiting.

PROJECT ARCHITECT Ken Shuttleworth
STRUCTURAL ENGINEER Ove Arup & Partners
SIZE 2950 square metres
CONTRACT VALUE £7.5 million
GETTING THERE from the south (London): exit 13 from the M1, turn right at roundabout, then first left following all signs to Cranfield University, first left at Salford, left at Cranfield Technology Park, next right to University. When you reach the reception building on campus ask how to get to the library
ACCESS announce yourself first at the main reception

Bedfordshire

Sir Norman Foster & Partners 1993

Bedfordshire

Sir Norman Foster & Partners 1993

East Anglia

Sheringham Leisure Pool

This was the practice's first major building in the UK – a fine display of distinctive and elegantly worked-out details given a relatively simple brief and a very tight budget. 'Splash' is located inland, away from the beaches and coastal paths. Its role is to evoke the pleasures of the beach without the hassles – sand in your sandwiches, umbrellas to keep off the rain, and changing into your swimsuit beneath a towel gripped between your teeth.

The building is quite conventional in plan and external appearance, but a closer look at the details reveals not just another light-industrial shed but thorough and inventive design. The roof is in two layers: a curved lid (with triangular corner hoppers for drainage) floating above two slanting side roofs. Rainwater on the lower roofs drains through tubes in the rafters into shiny silver, trumpet-shaped hoppers along each elevation. The external cladding was developed by the architects and is now a patented system. The two-layer hardwood with breather membrane comes in a standard sheet size, generating the grid of the building overall. The plywood panels are factory formed and erected on site – here there were three sections for each gable end and each of the long side elevations was erected in one section. Inside, timber lattice columns with tapered tops support bow-string trusses made of laminated timber, spanning 18.6 metres across the main pool space. Glu-lam beams (particularly appropriate for chemically sodden pool environments) span the side aisles.

The pool itself is sloped like a beach at one end with a wave machine; the main pool is 25 metres long so that it can be used for competitions. The changing area on the north side is made up of rows of beach huts with striped roofs. On the south side there is an orangery/café/terrace with balconies wound around the columns for views overlooking the pool. The east side accommodates the winter garden and conservatory for functions and is partitioned off from the pool area by a full-height glazed wall. The

Alsop Lyall & Störmer 1988

west end provides a plain backdrop for the spiralling water chute which is supported by a cantilevered bracket. A delicately balanced flight of steps once led you up to the top of the chute but they have been removed by the client. All the materials have been carefully chosen – conventional materials used in an imaginative way.

Public swimming pools have taken on an entirely new role in the 1980s – no longer just the local swimming baths for school parties, they are now leisure complexes, comparable with the shift made from shopping at local stores to going to out-of-town malls – a day out for the whole family. The architects have certainly risen to the occasion here by enhancing the spirit of holidays by the sea, without resorting to Disney tactics.

CLIENT North Norfolk District Council with The Clifford Barnett Group
STRUCTURAL ENGINEER Anthony Hunt Associates
SIZE 2800 square metres
CONTRACT VALUE £1.8 million
GETTING THERE on the northernmost coast of East Anglia, on the A149 Weybourne Road westward, following signs to the leisure pool
ACCESS open

Norfolk

Alsop Lyall & Störmer 1988

Norfolk/Suffolk

Alsop Lyall & Störmer 1988

Constable Terrace and Nelson Court
University of East Anglia, Norwich

Constable Terrace is a wall of student residences (the murky term 'hall of residence' does not apply here) and a flourish in the landscape at the University of East Anglia. Located directly north from and overlooking the celebrated Sainsbury Centre for the Visual Arts, the building elegantly snakes its way out of the west end of the campus. The eastern end is adjacent to Lasdun's Teaching Wall (1962–68) and Mather (consultant architect to the university) has added new pedestrian routes and a spine road to the original Lasdun masterplan.

Nelson Court, at the other end of the campus, is made up of more angular blocks making three sides of a courtyard and facing south, overlooking the lake. The core of the brief was a demand for extreme energy efficiency so that it would be cheap enough for students to rent during term time while attracting an upmarket clientele looking for decent overnight or conference accommodation during university holidays.

Until now the most popular student accommodation on the campus was some terraced houses built in 1979, each one catering for ten people. This size seemed to provide the right social balance so helped to inform Mather's scheme. A total of 800 rooms is arranged in ten-bedroom three-storey sections, each with their own main entrance, shared living room and well-equipped kitchen. They are sealed inside a sheer white external skin and here, at Constable Terrace, topped by a floating canopy roof. The potentially stark expanse of wall with flush windows is broken at pavement level by an intimate arrangement of minimal concrete seating on a terrace area in font of each glazed entrance/common room. As you walk by you can see yourself reflected full height against a reflection of the Sainsbury Centre, placing you in the landscape and welcoming you into Mather's building. Inside, the corridors flow like rivers and vertical

Norfolk

Rick Mather Architects 1994

Norfolk

Rick Mather Architects 1994

slivers of light like doors kept ajar create the feeling that there is always more space beyond. The bold central spiral staircase – encased in green mosaic and veiled in a bannister cage of vertical steel rods with a delicately balanced linking bridge above (with built-in wobble to make it feel all the more precarious) – is the perfect punctuation mark.

Perhaps more importantly, these student residences are the largest low-energy residential project in the UK to date. They are based on the proposition that even in winter the heat input required by each occupant would be a mere 250 watts (the equivalent of two light bulbs). With the skin sealed as tightly as possible, a mechanical system ventilates the interior – air is drawn in under the roof canopy and filters into each room at low level. The heat-recovery system captures about 70 per cent of the latent heat from extracted air and this is used to warm the fresh incoming air. Windows are fitted with low-emissivity glass and are the minimum size permitted under the Building Regulations. In the summer they can open to provide natural through draughts.

STRUCTURAL ENGINEER Dewhurst MacFarlane
SIZE Constable Terrace 9100 square metres; Nelson Court 9600 square metres
CONTRACT VALUE Constable Terrace £6.2 million; Nelson Court £6.6 million
GETTING THERE follow signs to the University of East Anglia, east from the centre of Norwich on the Earlham Road
ACCESS announce yourself to anyone in any of the lobbies in the block before you wander around

Norfolk

Rick Mather Architects 1994

Norfolk

Rick Mather Architects 1994

Sainsbury Centre for the Visual Arts and Crescent Wing

University of East Anglia, Norwich

Norfolk, with its huge skies, steely light and severed coastline, has the most architectural landscape that I have come across in this country. It invites an unashamed building form: there is nowhere for a building to hide in the unshrinking panorama. This may explain why this particular area embraces the stumpy verticality of its medieval parish churches as enthusiastically as some of the most rigorously modern buildings to have been built in Great Britain.

A major contribution to a continuously enlightened programme of modern building in the Norwich area is the determinedly research-based nature of East Anglia University. The entire campus is an architectural laboratory (one of the new 'plate-glass' universities – rather than the rabbit-hutch environments of the earlier red-brick universities), a 1960s' modernist response, masterplanned by Sir Denys Lasdun, to what was known as the Robin Principle (1959) which stated that everyone who could achieve the required qualifications was entitled to a university place. Both Sir Denys's stunning ziggurat halls of residence built from 1962 to 1968 and Foster's Sainsbury Centre for the Visual Arts built in 1977 (like a slab of marble rising out of the ground and fractured diagonally along its veins at each end) seem to grow out of this landscape.

It is impossible to look at the Crescent Wing extension without first looking at the siting and details of the original Sainsbury Centre. Built to house the Sir Robert and Lady Sainsbury Collection (including many works by Francis Bacon and Giacometti), it was sited on the axis of a new lake, a key part of the scheme that opened up a stunning view of the valley to the south. An integrated panel and primary structure enables any part of the external walls and roof to be changed quickly in order

Norfolk

Sir Norman Foster and Partners 1977–1991

Sir Norman Foster and Partners 1977–1991

to provide different combinations of glazed, solid or grilled aluminium panels. The entire inner wall and ceiling lining is a system of aluminium louvres which are motorised and linked to external and internal light sensors to provide a sophisticated control system. Artificial lighting on ceiling tracks eliminates disruption to the gallery layout. Services run between the wall surfaces in towers and trusses. The single large-span roof covers two exhibition galleries, a large reception area, the School of Fine Arts, a university faculty club, a public restaurant, and basement storage facilities. However, more space was required, primarily to house the best reserve-collection display in the world, and then to create a special gallery in which to teach museum lighting, and to provide conservation facilities for three-dimensional objects, an art transit room and additional offices and storage. This brief became the Crescent Wing.

The Sainsburys were adamant that the existing building should not be extended by extrusion, although its plan implied this as the obvious solution. It was decided that any extension would have to take place underground. The final plan was determined by the requirements of the brief. The fan shape accommodates the 200-capacity gallery (also to be used for conferences) more comfortably than the original rectilinear plan. The projection room is appropriately at the pointed end, the gallery in the fan shape and the offices are placed along the radial arc which emerges above ground, making a window out on to the lake. The study collection and laboratories fit along one arm of the fan.

The beauty of the extension is the way that it lies so discreetly in the landscape. Two minimal sculptural forms rather than a conventional building language tell you that something is lurking down there. The first is the entrance: a glazed slit in the level grass lawn with a slow decline into the ground, minimal handrail and an electronic sliding glass door

Norfolk

Sir Norman Foster and Partners 1977–1991

at the end. The second is the inclined, curved, glazed windscreen (to see it, walk towards the lake and look back at the main building). The only indication of its presence from the lawn above is, again, a handrail. This one is rather like a fence at a racecourse with an exaggerated curve. It shouts speed and flight!

The Crescent Wing is a stunning architectural feature in the landscape, the result of an entirely fresh look at how spaces can be organised internally (although the result is still somewhat claustrophobic in the route to and inside the gallery space due to an excess of carpet) and emphasising the key elements – entrance and window. However, if you talk to the security guards you get a different story – water runs down the entrance slope and under the electronic door; there is no alternative exit from that part of the building; and there is some questionable detailing in the wc – not irremediable problems, and they are being treated.

Visiting the Sainsbury Centre for Visual Arts and the Crescent Wing is thoroughly uplifting. Each element – the handrail, the breathtaking floating glass walkway link to the main campus, the bulk of the Sainsbury Centre building – is a powerful architectural statement: they contribute to the evolution of a landscape, and are not simply transferred on to it.

CLIENT Sir Robert and Lady Sainsbury
STRUCTURAL ENGINEER YRM Anthony Hunt Associates
SIZE Sainsbury Centre 6186 square metres; Crescent Wing 3000 square metres
GETTING THERE follow signs to the University of East Anglia, east from the centre of Norwich on the Earlham Road
ACCESS open during gallery hours, check times before you go

Norfolk

Sir Norman Foster and Partners 1977–1991

Norfolk

Sir Norman Foster and Partners 1977–1991

School of Occupational Therapy
University of East Anglia, Norwich

Richard Maxwell (*Architecture Today*) said this building 'has an aura of being careful of people'. What I think he means is that the building is not unnecessarily challenging – it is not a labyrinthine institutional block. Instead, it welcomes the human element, offering good communal and recreational facilities among the academic departments so that work and relaxation can interlock. Circulation and siting are major factors. Two and a half wings are focused around a grassy, tree-filled courtyard which slopes down to the south. The longest side forms an arcade on the ground-floor level, linking classrooms on the upper floors to the lecture hall and laboratories in the shorter southern wing, with the double-height glazed library next to a rendered block lifted on columns containing the gymnasium in the north wing. The entrance tower is a focal point, tucked into the south-west corner of the courtyard with common rooms on upper floors and a pharmacy on the lower ground floor.

The structure is set on a fair-faced blockwork plinth with white render above edged in a black brick trim as if the building had been drawn on to the site with a Magic Marker. Window frames are set into the walls, and cylindrical columns are plain. Venetian blinds hang externally on the west-facing windows and can be adjusted at the flick of a switch. This simplicity of detailing contributes to the building's repose.

STRUCTURAL ENGINEER F J Samuely & Partners
CLIENT Anglia and Oxford Health Authority
SIZE aproximately 3000 square metres
CONTRACT VALUE £3.3 million
GETTING THERE on the east side of Constable Terrace
ACCESS limited

Norfolk

John Miller & Partners 1993

Norfolk

John Miller & Partners 1993

Power Station
Eye

Here is one of the most exciting and dramatic approaches to any new building that I have encountered. The power station is sited at the end of a disused runway, in landscape like the plains of middle America. The power station itself is a glisteningly industrial steel-clad shed with a gently bowed roof. The form and size has been dictated entirely by the plant inside which was purpose-designed by Aalborg, a Danish firm of boiler-makers. The building is partially submerged by surrounding grassy banks, supposedly to reduce the impact of the building on the landscape. This seems both highly implausible and unnecessary.

However, the most interesting aspect of this building is why it is here at all. The power station, the first of its kind in Europe, will generate enough electricity to heat 10,000 homes from the litter of 100,000 battery chickens (half of Suffolk's annual poultry waste). The litter is burned at a very high temperature (850-1000° Celsius), producing steam to drive a turbine which in turn drives an electricity generator. The energy produced has a notably low level of polluting emissions. A by-product, 200 tonnes of ash is produced weekly and sold as nitrogen-free fertiliser.

CLIENT Fibropower Ltd
SIZE 1600 square metres
GETTING THERE A140 between Ipswich and Norwich, right turn to Eye
ACCESS clear view of the exterior; call Fibropower for an appointment to see inside

Suffolk

Lifschutz Davidson 1994

Suffolk

Lifschutz Davidson 1994

RNLI Lifeboat Station
Aldeburgh

Aldeburgh is definitely one of Britain's most beautiful and quaint villages. It is the home of the Aldeburgh Festival which takes place every summer, attracting classical-music lovers from all over the world. Sited on the beach directly opposite the Jubilee Hall, where the festival began, is the new Lifeboat Station, like two pitched rooftops pushing their way up through the pebbles. It is a bold statement and fits in well with the backdrop of elegantly jumbled houses on the seafront, made from brick, flint or painted timber, and the fishermen's huts and boats on either side. The building comprises a boat house and tractor shed linked by a public viewing gallery above the block containing crew facilities. The main design criterion was the integration of large doors for operational access with a small building mass.

The boat house and tractor shed are both A-frame structures made of stainless steel from which Glulam purlin beams are suspended, stablised by cables linking Glulam end caps to the apexes of the A-frames. Between the beams set beneath the apex of the frame is a low-pitched zinc roof, with steeply pitched slate sides following the roofline along the frame legs.

Internally, the ceiling is rough-sawn rafters with plywood lining. A frameless clerestory runs along the side elevations of the sheds, separating the roof with extended eaves from the red cedar-clad walls. These walls lean outward at approximately 5.5°, suggesting the bulging hull of a boat. The gable ends facing east towards the sea are glazed from the clerestory to the full height each side of central rolling garage doors. The whole structure sits on a concrete raft sunk below the surface level of the beach.

This is a very public building, welcoming visitors and encouraging them to explore every detail of its construction. The linking flat-roofed block is glazed on the sea frontage, with a public viewing terrace on top

Suffolk

Mullins Dowse and Partners 1994

Mullins Dowse and Partners 1994

reached from inside the boat house via a galvanised spiral stair. The landward side of the boat house has a viewing bridge stretching across its elevation.

It is also a very efficient structure, the A-frames allowing a column-free internal space for manoeuvering equipment and preparing the boat for a launch to be done without obstruction. The only obvious hazard is the underside of the spiral staircase with protruding edges at head height, now rectified by a liberal foam binding. The lifeboat house is proof that imaginative, good-quality detailing and therefore a significant building as a whole does not necessarily benefit from having a large budget thrown at it.

STRUCTURAL ENGINEER G C Robertson & Associates
CLIENT Royal National Lifeboat Institute
SIZE 300 square metres
CONTRACT VALUE £500,000 for the building, £1.5 million approximately for the building including the boat, tractor and all fitting-out materials and equipment
GETTING THERE on the beach close to the centre of Aldeburgh
ACCESS public viewing deck

Suffolk

Mullins Dowse and Partners 1994

Suffolk

Mullins Dowse and Partners 1994

J Sainsbury's Supermarket
Harlow

Another in Sainsbury's fleet. Their contribution says much about the shape of patronage in the 1990s – what might have been a Sunday drive to a stately home is now a trip to the stately superstore, and we can all share in the riches. At Harlow, the supermarket is located at the elbow of an L-shaped site. The south-east corner of the main shed is the primary feature and symbolises the supermarket as a popular cultural landmark: three large, white-rendered cubes, like milk cartons, projecting in front of and above the main store with blue enamelled drums sandwiched in between and revolving doors beneath. The cubes are arcaded beneath to store trolleys and the top corners have been punched out and painted bright primary colours so that at night they illuminate the bland landscape. Inside they house a chemist, a newsagent and lavatories. The pedestrian cycleway that previously crossed the site has been retained on a new bridge that bisects the car park and forms a link with the centre of town.

The north elevation (staff entrance) has also been given a public face. The elevation has the grandeur and symmetry of a major public building, with steps leading up to a large central entrance window set in a white stucco wall, flanked by chequerboard blockwork and blue towers. Its role is to express the importance and impact of Sainsbury's as a major player in the world of commerce while the customer entrance capitalises on the lure of trusted 'own-brand' packaging.

STRUCTURAL ENGINEER Ernest Green Partnership
GETTING THERE on the north edge of Harlow bordered by Hammarskjold Road to the north, Fifth Avenue to the east, Fourth Avenue to the south and Hodings Road (leading into Rectory Wood) to the west
ACCESS open

Essex

Terry Farrell & Company 1994

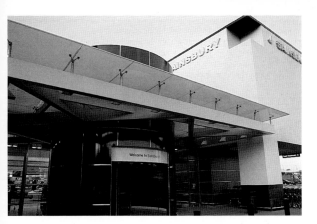

Essex

Terry Farrell & Company 1994

Stansted Airport

There has been a runway at Stansted since 1942. In 1953 Stansted was singled out as London's potential third airport. Forty years and several public inquiries, reports, and committees later, the new terminal was opened by HM the Queen. Foster Associates became involved in the project in 1981. During the long gaps while decisions were being made in Whitehall the time was used positively to develop a good relationship with the client.

The main design concept for the airport derived from Foster's own love of flying (he would travel to the site, stress-free, in his own helicopter) and the simplicity of early airport terminals. The open fields of Stansted invited a low, single-storey building with a roadside entrance and car park on one side and the runway and aeroplane satellites on the other.

Travellers by rail arrive underneath the building and are transported via an escalator or lifts directly into the main concourse. Check-in, shops, security areas and departure lounge are arranged in a linear fashion to avoid excessive signage and disorientation, with views onto the runway. A monorail shuttle whisks passengers to the adjacent satellite for boarding. This ease of passage was greatly informed by many hours spent in airports whilst the architects flew back and forth from Hong Kong during the construction of the Hong Kong & Shanghai Bank.

The vast open space of the main building is clearly articulated by the spectacular roof structure which floats more than 15 metres above our heads. A quilt of square domes is supported by a grid of 36 service trees. The white roof membrane (perforated steel trays and insulated Sarnafil PVC) filters light down onto the grey terrazzo floor and reflects light from inside. The domes also act as smoke reservoirs with extractor fans built into the top of each tree. Another significant achievement in the design of the roof is the syphonic draining system which allows drainpipes to

Essex

Essex

Foster Associates 1985–91

be laid horizontally. All air-conditioning, information and lighting services are contained in the roof support/service pods, leaving the concourse space completely free of pipes and ducts. Travellers and airport staff can see the sky, the 'planes and the fields through the glazed perimeter walls all around. Remarkably, a highly technical and structurally sophisticated enclosure exudes the qualities of a natural environment.

Interior detailing was never treated as a separate issue as far as the architects were concerned. Everything from carpets and seating to check-in desks has been dealt with obsessively, each item having been custom-made for this particular terminal. Even the white, fire-proof retail 'cabins' have been rigorously designed so that they disguise loud shop logos and unsightly trad brass fittings. Check-in desks are made from a kit of stainless steel and linoleum-covered plywood parts that can be rearranged easily as more airlines move to Stansted.

It is anticipated that 8 million passengers a year will pass through the terminal by the end of this century, and there will be space to accommodate 15 million in the future. I hope that the surrounding infrastructure, the road and rail links, provide the necessary back-up.

STRUCTURAL ENGINEER Ove Arup & Partners
CLIENT British Airports Authority/Stansted Airport Ltd
CONTRACT VALUE £400 million
SIZE main terminal is 39,000 square metres
GETTING THERE by road: just off M11; by rail: regular train service from Liverpool Street and Tottenham Hale
ACCESS open

Essex

Foster Associates 1985–91

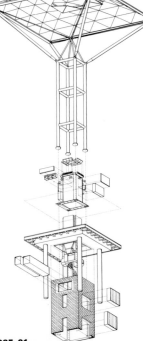

Essex

Foster Associates 1985–91

Berkshire, Wiltshire, Gloucestershire

Imperium
Reading

This office development was Bennetts Associates' first major building and they were duly rewarded with National and Regional RIBA Awards in 1991. When the A33 is complete, Imperium will stand as the first major building to be seen on the approach into Reading.

The project started shortly after the then Secretary of State for the Environment, Nicholas Ridley, relaxed planning controls on office developments in areas designated for industrial use. Business/industrial parks began to spring up on the outskirts of Britain's cities in the 1980s. Like out-of-town shopping, out-of-town working has become all the rage. What remains in town is discussed elsewhere in this book.

The building is simple in plan: two three-storey deep-plan office spaces flank a central atrium, approached via a raised walkway over a waterfall and pool. The water seems to flow through the building as a large glazed panel beneath the walkway reflects it into the basement car park. The entire atrium is glazed (roof and front façade), creating a dazzling interior space which achieves an outdoor scale. Internal materials echo the external pure white silo/barn-like shapes of the office blocks. A polished stone floor, timber wall-linings and landscaping internally and externally soften the severe industrial surroundings.

The office spaces themselves are glazed all the way around with views into the atrium, uncluttered at present. The adjacent car park has been planted with trees arranged on the same grid as the columns in the building, gradually evolving as an urban orchard – cars shelter under the trees like grazing livestock.

Imperium's own boundaries are clearly defined although it tries hard to root itself in the industrial landscape on its heavy black brick base. The architect has tried to marry the two scales by introducing water and gently

Berkshire

Bennetts Associates Architects 1987–89

rolling lawns into the immediate surroundings, and enveloping the sky through the atrium and gently curving roof lines. This building is clearly made for its occupants, whereas its industrial neighbours are built for the products.

CLIENT Speyhawk Land & Estates
STRUCTURAL ENGINEER Franks & Lewin
SIZE 10,000 square metres
CONTRACT VALUE £9.3 million
GETTING THERE take junction 11 off the M4 going west,
Imperium, Worton Drive, Worton Grange, is sited in the first industrial estate on your right-hand side as you head north into Reading on Imperial Way (look out for the Courage Brewery which is beyond on adjoining land)
ACCESS to industrial estate only

Berkshire

Bennetts Associates Architects 1987–89

Bennetts Associates Architects 1987–89

The Anvil Arts Centre
Basingstoke

The Anvil Arts Centre has provided a new social centre for the town. Its auditorium can rise to any one of four occasions: proscenium-arched theatre, arena, concert hall and banqueting hall. By its own versatility it takes on the role of town hall which is also enhanced by its location. The building is situated between the main shopping centre and the main arterial road, and can be approached on foot over a new red steel footbridge from the railway station. All the routes meet in front of a two-storey red drum containing the box office and VIP room. The main auditorium sits on a diagonal, the steel-clad plant tower protruding as the hard nose of the creature. It is slightly detached in order to isolate noise of the plant equipment from the auditorium. Internally, the dislocation has created an irragularly shaped, double-height foyer space, lit by a full-height window opening out on to a terrace café in summer.

The flexibility of the auditorium is of primary interest. The front seven rows of seats disappear beneath the floor on an elevator. The middle row of ten seats is electrically retractable. The proscenium arch and film screen are contained in a rising and pivoting floor section in the platform. The whole auditorium has a double-skin upper wall and roof, like a buffer zone stopping noise infiltrating the space. The aural reflectors inside the space, set beneath the main roof trusses, form a cornice and are painted colours that can be found in Rothko's paintings.

STRUCTURAL ENGINEER Whitby & Bird
CLIENT Basingstoke and Dean Borough Council
SIZE 14,000 square metre auditorium seating 1400
GETTING THERE
ACCESS open

Hampshire

RHWL 1994

Hampshire

RHWL 1994

Renault Distribution Centre
Swindon

Swindon is not exactly a tourist centre, and its industrial hinterland is the car-salesroom capital of the country, but this is one project that is worth travelling to see. The generating influence for this magnificent building is the structural module – a masted, lightweight, suspended roof that repeats in an omni-directional pattern – four bays wide and eleven bays long. There are 27 masts and 360 tie rods. Each bay of the roof is like an inverted umbrella, 24 metres square, hung on a 16-metre-high tubular steel mast positioned on a 30-metre grid. The lowest points of the roof are 9.5 metres from ground level, creating a large clear span inside the shed. The loading on one bay effects the performance of other neighbouring bays, the whole roof absorbing all loads with expansion joints or structural connections where it meets the walls.

There are many intersections between beams, tension rods, smoke outlets and glazed skylights. It is the conscientious detailing in these areas that makes this an important building rather than just an expressionistic industrial unit. The roof decking is 100-mm-deep corrugated steel with an acoustic lining in the office and showroom areas at the front. A 75-mm layer of mineral-wool sheet insulation is laid across the top and covered with a continuous sheet of solvent-welded PVC with PVC-coated metal sections at the junctions between roof and walls. At each intersection, where a column or tension rod pierces the roof, a solvent-bonded PVC binding or sleeve is sealed around it. Planar glazing rooflights are bolted onto PVC-coated metal sections with a sealed Neoprene gasket between the two.

The rigid non-structural screen walls (glass in the showroom area) do not naturally reconcile themselves with the supple nature of the roof. Employing technology based on the tie-down fixings used to prevent the

Foster Associates 1983

Wiltshire

Foster Associates 1983

flapping and tearing of fabric-sided trucks, a 350-mm black Neoprene gasket is loosely fitted between bolted channel seams at the tops of the walls and underneath the eaves. Stainless-steel coil springs are stretched from halfway up the gasket down to the wall channel. This is a practical design solution, but the aesthetic effect is very satisfying, enhancing the lightness of the structure by tying rather than bolting. Needless to say, the roof still leaks in places but I wonder if that has more to do with maintenance than accurate detailing?

The open front canopy and glazed reception area reveal the roof pattern – you can see how it inspired the roof at Stansted Airport (see page 226), also by Foster – a square with a central skylight panel and diagonal corner bracing, although here the roof is suspended from the top and at Stansted it is rooted to central columns. The front lobby is an enormous and stunning space with a clear 180° view through armour-plated glass (4-metre-square sheets are bolted in just eight places).

The only features occupying the space are four skeleton car bodies flying overhead, an unfortunate reception desk (replacing the original Foster-designed Nomos table – although these can still be found in the staff cafeteria) with dried-flower arrangement dwarfed in the corner. Specially designed heating units are cantilevered at a low level off the floor and fixed to thin steel columns. The casing, which looks like a rocket booster, encloses a water-fed radiator and a fan to discharge warm air.

A diagonal stair leads up to a second level of offices, each bay faced with an industrial roller-shutter blind to reinforce the idea of 'production line' – in fact this building simply stores and distributes car parts. The detailing of each building element – glass doors, where the building meets the ground, where the concrete floorplates float behind the glazed walls (suspended ceiling added later in cafeteria) – has been treated with equal

Wiltshire

Foster Associates 1983

attention.

The promenade along the uncovered arcade on the east side of the building wraps you in the structure and scale of what feels like precision, machine-made, architectural landscaping.

STRUCTURAL ENGINEER Ove Arup & Partners
CLIENT Renault UK Limited
SIZE 25,000 square metres
CONTRACT VALUE £8.5 million
GETTING THERE follow signs to West
Swindon, past the Link Centre on the
right. Turn right at next roundabout,
past the de Vere Hotel and Pizza Hut on
the left, signs to the Meads; go straight on
and you can't miss it on your left-hand
side
ACCESS very limited inside but visitors are
free to walk around outside

Wiltshire

Foster Associates 1983

Wiltshire

Foster Associates 1983

Oxfordshire

Ice Rink
Oxford

It is interesting to see how an architect develops over his or her career but there are very few in this country whose work can be observed consistently – so many build abroad or rarely build at all. Grimshaw is an exception: he has built widely here and has tackled a variety of building types. Structural expression and the support of wide spans are Grimshaw signatures (see Sainsbury's in Camden, London). This ice rink is an early example in the development of these themes. The ground is filled so it has a low load-bearing capacity. A central spine spans 73.2 metres, picking up more than 50 per cent of the roof load. Beams positioned at 15-metre intervals are supported by groups of four stainless-steel tension rods which hang from two 457-mm-diameter, 33-metre-high steel masts. The masts are stabilised by tie rods anchored to tension piles, 12.32 metres away from each mast.

Walls are heavily insulated cold-store panels coated in silver PVC. The roof is galvanised steel sheeting riveted to the underside of metal decking. The north face is triple-glazed entirely in Kappafloat glass with an internal adjustable louvre system – so there is a clear view inside from Oxpens Road (see the Financial Times Printworks, London Docklands). As in later projects by Grimshaw, the elements of this building are vast in scale. His buildings are frequently described as engineering feats whereas much is an over-compensation and exaggeration of structural parts.

STRUCTURAL ENGINEER Ove Arup & Partners
CLIENT Oxford City Council
SIZE 3000 square metres
GETTING THERE Oxpens Road, Oxford
ACCESS open

Oxfordshire

Nicholas Grimshaw & Partners 1984

Oxfordshire

Nicholas Grimshaw & Partners 1984

Bowra Building, Wadham College
Oxford

'The intention of the Bowra building is to reaffirm the collegiate character of Wadham and to find an appropriate response to its history and to its original architecture without losing the authenticity of the present': Richard MacCormac. The practice has had extensive experience of designing sensible and robust university buildings and this one is no exception. The tight site is close to the brown glazed gable end of the 1970s' library block designed by Andy MacMillan and Isi Metzstein and defines the back boundary of the college on probably its last available piece of land. It provides student accommodation and related facilities which can also be used for conference lettings and foreign student accommodation during holidays. MacCormac openly acknowledges the source of inspiration – Hardwick Hall by Robert Smythson (1590–97) – by producing a building which has 'more glass than wall'. This may be apparent from the inside because of the amount of natural light which manages to penetrate the building, and from the student comments that there is not enough poster-hanging space, but the layered forms of brick with stone quoining on the exterior give the reverse impression.

The plan is based around a central linear street above ground level. Ground level is occupied by services, kitchens, a gymnasium and squash court, communal rooms and a bar that overlooks the garden. Residential space is on the new raised street level and arranged around dog-leg stairs inside protruding towers which wriggle up out of the cramped site. Garret-like study bedrooms at the top have views over the city skyline and are within chatting distance of neighbouring towers. Two sides of the street face each other in close proximity, capturing the feeling of the narrow streets in the old part of town, exaggerated further by the large thresholds positioned at the entrance to each stack of rooms.

Oxfordshire

MacCormac Jamieson Prichard 1992

Oxfordshire

The buildings are made up of a series of sociable spaces which should increase chance meetings. The layering of the spaces helps to reduce the building bulk and the minimally abstracted details create bold shapes, dissecting the symmetrical front and rear elevations. From the side the symmetry is broken by curved bay windows on the corners – a device used in English Baroque country houses where front and back elevations were different but symmetrical with the sides apparently sandwiched irregularly in between. The pattern and materials are densely packed so that as you walk along the street you feel like you are climbing through rooftops. This contrasts successfully with the light and airy interiors.

STRUCTURAL ENGINEER Moore Vaughan MacLean and Partners
CLIENT Wadham College
SIZE 3500 square metres
CONTRACT VALUE £5.5 million
GETTING THERE Parks Road, Oxford
ACCESS interior by appointment only

Oxfordshire

MacCormac Jamieson Prichard 1992

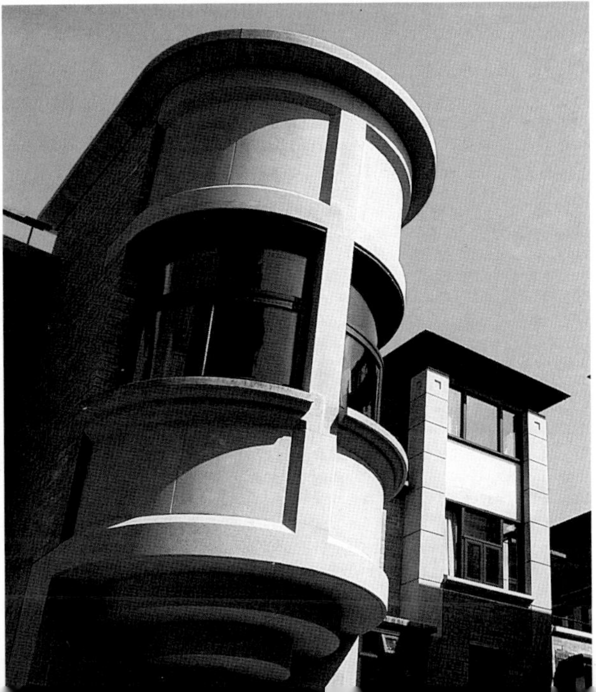

St John's College Garden Quad
Oxford

A continuation of the train of thought behind the Bowra Building at Wadham College (see page 220) by the same architects: a series of rectilinear towers protruding from a new ground level (garden terraces), with communal activities below in a cavernous undercroft. It is also a display of the wide range of formations and finishes that can be achieved using concrete. The creamy white concrete used here is made from a mixture of Derbyshire limestone and Portland cement, polished in some areas to shine like marble and rough cut elsewhere to look like broken stone. As the engineer explained, concrete was inevitable because it was the 'only material capable of making the forms that articulated the structure and its function'. Most of the elements are pre-cast blocks and beams put together very carefully, with particular attention paid to the joints, where staining might occur in the future.

The quad occupies a narrow site at the back of St John's (as at Wadham, it is the last patch of ground on which the college can build). The approach is via a covered cloister which runs along the south side of the undercroft and leads you into the central open-air courtyard. There is an auditorium on one side and a dining room on the other – both covered by 8.6-metre-diameter shallow domes made of 175-mm-thick in-situ concrete with a central pre-cast lantern protruding up to the garden terrace above.

The open courtyard has a notional dome of the same proportions as the other two but the roof has been sliced away. Here can be seen clearly how the domes are supported – on 8.2 tonne pre-cast concrete pendentives (curved corner brackets), each carried on four pre-cast concrete column clusters standing, in turn, on a plinth. Spanning between are eight arched cantilevered beams carried on L-shaped columns set behind the pendentives. These arches are highly polished surfaces resting on rusti-

MacCormac Jamieson Prichard 1993

Oxfordshire

MacCormac Jamieson Prichard 1993

cated bases. The rustication extends to the interior spaces on this level, enriching the underground atmosphere. The span is low and wide, creating a feeling of a large expanse of space while remaining secure and cloistered – Oriental in its proportions and spatial quality, Italian Renaissance in its detailing and Modernist in its geometry.

The garden terrace above is Italianate, with a series of vistas up to it and a geometrical pattern of pathways around stepped planted areas with built-in seating. The two lanterns from the rooms below project up through the terraces and become garden follies. The planting is soft and tumbling to contrast with the hard edges of the pre-cast concrete.

The terrace is surrounded on three sides by the accommodation towers, two to three storeys high. They are made of load-bearing brick and masonry with in-situ concrete floors. The rooms are arranged around traditional spiral stairs, as found in the old colleges. The south-facing rooms are stunning, extremely generous split-level, double-height spaces; sophisticated Corbusian apartments, surrounded with glass to admit as much natural light as possible. Unfortunately, this creates a tremendous build-up of heat and the ventilation is not sufficient to cope. For example, bedroom windows on the balcony level only open about 10 cm because of a blind rail positioned directly behind. To add insult to injury, the glass in this window is opaque so the blinds are redundant. Surely good ventilation in a student's bedroom is of prime importance – the two-week-old piles of laundry and the pizza boxes left lying around from the weekend before need a decent airing. The shower room is even more surprising – a tight arrangement of one door opening on to a shower door (fitted so closely together that it is impossible not to pinch your fingers between the frame and the internal glass door) without a transition from the corridor into the shower cubicle. There is no lobby area in which to hang

MacCormac Jamieson Prichard 1993

Oxfordshire

MacCormac Jamieson Prichard 1993

your towel or dry your feet. Again, the ventilation is not powerful enough so mildew is beginning to grow. The cramped dressing 'shelf' reminds me of the trying experience of changing into your clothes while wrapped in a towel on the beach. The shared kitchen is on a landing level and is also cramped, with too many double fire doors (now propped open with forks) to negotiate.

It is remarkable that the exterior and the undercroft rooms show such generosity and sensitivity towards the spaces, yet in dealing with the key element of the building, the accommodation, the architects have resorted to an old-school approach to the basic functional needs of day-to-day life.

Oxfordshire

STRUCTURAL ENGINEER Price & Myers
CLIENT St John's College
SIZE 3200 square metres
CONTRACT VALUE £7.5 million
GETTING THERE St Giles
ACCESS open, but you need an appointment to get inside

MacCormac Jamieson Prichard 1993

Oxfordshire

MacCormac Jamieson Prichard 1993

Linacre College
Oxford

Two very ordinary-looking residences have been built to house the ever-increasing number of students that the city council insists the university accepts each year. They are red-brick buildings with mock-Queen Anne façades and a dash of Dutch gabling, styles dictated by the city planners. However this project is one of the 'greenest 'developments of recent years. It has been rated by the Building Research Establishment Environmental Assessment Method due to the low-energy design, focusing on the environmental impact of the materials, that is, their 'embodied energy' – the energy consumed in their production rather than the energy that the building will use, although the two ultimately go hand in hand.

From an extensive list, the features that the architects believe are unique to the project are the greywater recycling system (bath and basin water, and filtered rainwater fed into cisterns), the embodied energy within materials used, i.e. natural materials, and the decision to offset the carbon-dioxide emissions implied by gas and electricity use (more than 42 tonnes a year) by adopting 40 acres of threatened Tasmanian eucalyptus forest. The buildings look ordinary, but they constitute an entire living and breathing system – isn't it time now that the form and the details evolve at the same rate as the organs, rather than resorting to a cosmetic-surgery job determined by the planners?

STRUCTURAL ENGINEERS Curtain Consulting Engineers
CLIENT Linacre College
SIZE 986 square metres
CONTRACT VALUE £2 million
GETTING THERE St Cross Road, Oxford
ACCESS appointment only

Oxfordshire

ECD Partnership 1994

Clare Palley Building, St Anne's College
Oxford

The Clare Palley Building represents a new generation of university buildings which double up as conference centres during holidays, offering lecture- and concert-hall facilities. The more comfortable and hotel-like the environment, the wealthier the clients will be – an influential consideration here.

St Anne's was the first Oxford college to offer a university education to women and the first women's college to admit men. It has a motley collection of buildings to its name – an administration block by Sir Giles Gilbert Scott (1938), a fine dining hall by Gerald Banks (1959), and a gatehouse and halls of residence by Howell, Killick, Partridge and Amis. (1966). These buildings surround three sides of a quad, the fourth side being bordered by a scattering of listed Victorian houses which also belong to the college. In the middle is the new block which cuts across the tree-filled garden to enclose a smaller lawned and flower-bedded garden next to the perimeter wall.

The building is L-shaped in plan with the three-storey residential block forming one arm (opposite the Gilbert Scott building) and the two-storey lecture hall forming the other.

The client wanted a building that would last for 200 years and appear to be mature from day one. This determined the materials used – hand-made bricks, Stoke Ground stone, Westmorland slate and oak for the walls, cornices, roof and joinery respectively. The first two floors of the accommodation block are in brick with horizontal bands of stone coursing and oak bay windows. In order to reduce the impact of the third floor and to keep in line with the lower lecture-hall wing, this level has been clad in oak panelling, slightly set back from the top cornice, and

Alec French Partnership 1993

Oxfordshire

Alec French Partnership 1993

the roof is set further back so that it is invisible from the ground. The horizontal stone bands continue around the apex of the building to wrap the two wings together. This corner apex forms the main entrance with a double-height glazed wall set in oak frames. Inside the lobby a mezzanine level takes you into the 150-seat auditorium; alternatively you can access the stage end through the carpeted conservatory to the right.

The interiors are small and claustrophobic, with a lot of carpet, oak joinery wherever you turn and little natural light in the central corridors of the accommodation block. To break the monotony of one long corridor it has been divided, providing two stairwell access points along the north face. Glazed on all storeys on the outside, solid walls divide the space internally rather than leaving open light wells and the possibility of a communal space.

To make rooms more enticing to visitors, each one is fitted with a bathroom and this reduces the size of the study rooms considerably. Too much has been sacrificed to the requirements of the building's holiday occupants – if I were a student coming to spend three of the best years of my life here I would feel I had been consigned to an old people's home.

STRUCTURAL ENGINEER Kenneth Brown and Partners
CLIENT St Anne's College
SIZE 1220 square metres
CONTRACT VALUE £1.56 million
GETTING THERE on the Woodstock Road north out of Oxford city centre
ACCESS by appointment only

Oxfordshire

Alec French Partnership 1993

Oxfordshire

Alec French Partnership 1993

Solid State Logic
Begbroke

Solid State Logic make sound- and vision-mixing equipment, those enormous desks in recording studios covered in thousands of buttons and sliders. This is one of Michael Hopkins' most successful projects. The practice was commissioned to design a building to house the manufacturing operation on the ground floor and the research, development and testing department on the first floor. The plan is square with a central top-lit atrium linking the two floors. From the outside the entire building is steel and glass with a flat roof. The grey tint in the glass moderates the solar heat gain, partially obscuring views in and out of the building. Excessive solar heat gain is prevented by fully retractable, remote-controlled external blinds (responding intelligently to changing light levels) mounted between subsidiary columns on the first-floor ... well, that was the idea. Rapidly changing light levels meant that the blinds were retracting and unfolding at such a pace that occupants were driven to distraction. The system has been switched off and individuals now control their own light levels.

The cantilevered first floor provides permanent shading from high summer sun to the ground floor and creates a narrow colonnade around the perimeter of the building. Full-height sliding glass doors on both floors mean that 50 per cent of the enclosure can open up, providing natural ventilation to a very deep floor plan. The diagonal staircases unfold from two opposite elevations, defining the immediately surrounding outdoor spaces as part of the whole structure.

The interior has changed radically since the initial brief was executed. The in-situ concrete first-floor slab has shallow coffered domes on the underside to hold light fittings (see the development of this technique at the Inland Revenue in Nottingham, page 128), and is supported on

Oxfordshire

Michael Hopkins & Partners 1988

Oxfordshire

Michael Hopkins & Partners 1988

slender hollow-section steel columns with a fire-protective coating – this remains untouched. But the central atrium, with its ceiling of open and closed panels to aid passive ventilation, once designated as a communal space, is now overrun with partitions, equipment and electronic parts. The law regarding the extraction of solder fumes recently changed so the clients have run grey plastic plumbing pipe from each workbench to an extractor on the outside, adding an interesting new haphazard dimension to the rigid geometry and precision of detailing that was initially set out by the architect. Upstairs, partitions have been inserted and as a result additional artificial lighting has become necessary.

From the outside the building maintains a distinctive modern air, floating like a pavilion in parkland.

STRUCTURAL ENGINEER Buro Happold
CLIENT Solid State Logic
SIZE ground plan is 43.2 by 43.2 metres
GETTING THERE A44 to Woodstock, on Springhill Road behind the Royal Sun pub on your left after the Begbroke sign
ACCESS by appointment only

Oxfordshire

Michael Hopkins & Partners 1988

Michael Hopkins & Partners 1988

Henley Royal Regatta Headquarters

The Terry Farrell Partnership is well known as a champion of post-modernism with large projects in London such as the development at Embankment Place, the huge office block in Vauxhall for MI6, and abroad with large urban redevelopment schemes, but back in the home counties is a small project that was a forerunner of these grand schemes. The site is on the riverfront at Henley-on-Thames, a town which comes to life once a year in the summer for the Henley Royal Regatta - the world-renowned rowing event and a major social occasion.

A vast pediment set on a similarly proportioned brick plinth (respecting the scale of the adjacent stone bridge), the building is a temple of Classical elements transformed into exaggerated modern forms. The ground floor of the headquarters accommodates the main entrance on the north-facing side, offices, a grand hall and a committee room facing west, overlooking the river. This façade is articulated by a tall Venetian window breaking through a pediment above. All the rooms on this floor have differing ceiling heights, establishing a hierarchy of spaces. The boat-house is underneath, and on the top floor is an apartment for the regatta secretary, with skylights in the roof and dormer windows. Wood and stucco painted bright colours disguise the inadequacy of the structure and materials used. However, the exterior does not do justice to the disciplined organisation of spaces inside, which makes maximum use of limited space.

STRUCTURAL ENGINEER Peter Brett Associates
CLIENT Henley Royal Regatta
GETTING THERE over Henley Bridge, Henley-on-Thames
ACCESS limited

Oxfordshire

Terry Farrell Partnership 1985

Terry Farrell Partneship 1985

Dorset, Devon, Cornwall

Poundbury
Dorchester

This guide shows you the latest developments in the pattern of building in England; this is not an interpolated lesson in the history of rural vernacular architecture. Believe it or not, this development represents the latest trend in rural planning. This is how we should be living in the 21st century, according to Prince Charles – a development that he hopes will signal the demise of monotonous housing estates and revive the traditional character of England's suburbs. The plans were first unveiled in 1989 and now phase 1, section A is near completion, boasting 26 two to five-bedroom houses. A two-bedroom flat in a mock-Georgian terrace house costs £80,000; £200,000 buys a five-bedroom detached mock-Victorian workers' cottage.

The design rules for the buildings were devised by the architects of Seaside, Florida, and were tested by Rob Krier at Vienna University. His students made a 1:100 model of the village, specifying heights, styles of window, and types of local materials – brick, stucco, slate and tile. Each property is a direct copy of existing buildings from a range of stylistic periods, adorned with extras such as a Victorian carriage lamp, a rubbish-bin pen, a garage (like a large dog kennel) and a modern interior *á la* MFI. The line was drawn at thatched roofs as they were considered to be 'too twee'. A local architect told me that he 'would not have passed the properties for council house standards inside.' To keep within the budget many features were scrapped along the way: secondary glazing was replaced by cheaper double glazing, open fires and chimneys were rejected and fewer 'unusually' shaped houses were put forward.

The overall planning of the estate is fundamentally impaired by the overriding focus on car-parking space rather than public space. The hindquarters of the present group of houses back onto a car park and garages,

Dorset

Leon Krier (masterplan) 1993–94

Dorset

Leon Krier (masterplan) 1993–94

replacing what could have been a large communal garden. Some of the houses have pokey back yards.

The next stage of the plan does not look any more hopeful – a marginal widening of a street lined on one side with terraced houses is labelled 'the square'. The children living in these first-phase houses have resorted to riding their bikes round and round the car park in monotonous circles. Once they step outside their cloister they meet acres of beautiful countryside on one side, the main road on another and grim faces pressed up against the fences on the other two sides. These belong to the families who live in the less desirable neighbouring estates – they are fed up with the attention that Poundbury (known locally as Monkey's Jump) receives. Dust and noise from the ongoing building programme wafts into their houses day in and day out and meanwhile the walls between classes are built higher and higher.

The land allocated for each house was cut in the first phase because Dorset council insisted that the development be commercially viable and address the immediate needs of the community. This increased the housing density at Poundbury from 330 to 450 homes and increased the car-parking facilities for tourists and shoppers. An obscure 19th century law means that the Treasury can block the use of Duchy funds, so the architects and planners really had no choice but to comply!

The masterplanners sought to avoid a road-dominated suburban layout. Ironically, Poundbury's real village centre is 5 km away on the ring road link with the south side of Dorchester. It is the brand new Tesco superstore on the A354 coming into Dorchester, which means that residents of Poundbury do not have to venture into the old town centre at all. This Tesco's is the most ostentatious that I have seen. It has taken on town-hall status with its vast steep-pitched roofs, dormer windows, clock

Dorset

Leon Krier (masterplan) 1993–94

Leon Krier (masterplan) 1993–94

and bell tower and, grandest of all, fountains, hanging baskets and steps up to … the side of the building. The main entrance is on the adjacent car-park side. The brick column colonnade around the perimeter of the supermarket has stone capitals decorated with carved animal heads. There must be enough timber signage scattered around to build several log cabins.

Next door is the new football stadium, designed in the style of … Tesco's! It blends in perfectly with the surrounding scale and style of architecture – Prince Charles must feel proud. In association with the supermarket barons, he has promoted the transformation of life in suburban Dorchester into a 'public convenience'. The consequences of this are alarming – exciting modern concepts such as ease, comfort and accessibility are shrouded in 'olde worlde' apparel. The architects are simply not telling the truth.

ASSOCIATED ARCHITECTS Percy Thomas Partnership/Ken Morgan Associates
STRUCTURAL/CIVIL ENGINEER Aspley Associates
LANDSCAPE ARCHITECT Adrian Lisney and Partners
CLIENT Duchy of Cornwall
SIZE 160 hectares in total
CONTRACT VALUE first phase £4 million
GETTING THERE A35 west following signs to Bridport out of Dorchester town centre, past hospital on left, up a hill, down the other side and you will meet a roundabout – the site is ahead on your left side
ACCESS open, although homes are private

Dorset

Leon Krier (masterplan) 1993–94

Leon Krier (masterplan) 1993–94

Hooke Park
Beaminster

Hooke Park is 134 hectares of woodland. The three-humped structure is the training centre, and now a commercial workshop. To the right is a prototype house. The buildings are monumental demonstrations of a unique construction technique that uses low-grade Norway Spruce thinnings – the spindly trees that are pulled up and burnt as waste in order to let the healthiest trees grow bigger for good-quality timber. John Makepeace, furniture maker and founder of the Parnham Trust School of fine furniture design, discovered that 3.5 million tonnes of thinnings were being destroyed in this country every year, but that their bending potential was so immense that structures could be made with whole uncut timbers, resulting in little or no waste. The diameter of a thinning is no more than 50 mm at one end and 150 mm at the other. Frei Otto, Richard Burton and William Moorwood of Ahrends Burton Koralek, and Ted Happold were commissioned to develop the scheme for the buildings because of their knowledge of tension and compression structures.

The house was built first. A tension structure, it is raised off the ground and incorporates a new kind of joint – a conical hole is drilled into the end of the timber and filled with epoxy resin, a threaded steel rod is beaded into the resin and connected to the next timber. The building timbers are so rigid that the tensioning cables added to stabilise any movement in the wood are now completely slack. The windows lean out diagonally over the undergrowth and bases of trees and prove to be well suited to people in wheelchairs as they reveal views outside without any straining of necks.

The training centre is a lattice shell made up of a series of arches joined by horizontal timber bands and covered with a Sarnafil skin. The timber is treated with boron salt solution. A skylight runs along the top ridge, allowing light into the belly-like space. The curve in it makes it extremely

Frei Otto, Buro Happold, Ahrends Burton Koralek 1986–89

Frei Otto, Buro Happold, Ahrends Burton Koralek 1986–89

hot and dazzling at certain times of the day, especially in the office area. Panels each side of the skylight inflate and deflate for natural ventilation.

The buildings take on unconventional shapes and an unconventional aesthetic. They result from the logic of the structure, surely the purest form of architecture, at the same time cultivating a new vernacular. The next stage is to develop the skins, fittings and light sources. Research is also being carried out on new materials, using the thinnings and other waste timber and applying principles used in aircraft technology to develop lightweight construction materials – the present workshop manager has extensive experience in high-tech aircraft design. The workshop is beginning to design its own range of furniture in order to make the place commercially viable, and courses are run for groups of students on the use of renewable local resources, preservation, stresses in timbers, load-bearing qualities, joints, weather-proofing and how to translate all this information into a good working environment.

In 1993 Edward Cullinan was commissioned to design five houses for students on the campus, using the local second-grade timber. They are to be designed for standard commercial demands, such as a two-bedroom starter home, and the target is that a house be self-built in just two days. If it takes 21 days to build a Boeing 747 from start to first take off, this seems quite feasible … watch this space.

STRUCTURAL ENGINEER Buro Happold
CLIENT Hooke Forest Construction acting for the Parnham Trust
GETTING THERE B3163 from Beaminster towards the A356, second turn on right to Hooke, along lane; the entrance on the right is shown by two large circular tree sculptures
ACCESS open

Dorset

Frei Otto, Buro Happold, Ahrends Burton Koralek 1986–89

Frei Otto, Buro Happold, Ahrends Burton Koralek 1986–89

J Sainsbury's Supermarket
Marsh Mills, Plymouth

It is impossible to miss this flagship supermarket building as you come into Plymouth on the elevated section of the A38 where it meets the head of the Plym Estuary. The site is bounded to the south by the London–Plymouth railway line so it has a tremendous prominence from all angles.

The architects claim that the design of the project centres around the car park, which seems to make good sense as superstore grocery shopping is now very much the late 20th-century norm. They also suggest that this could be 'a romantic landscape proposal … with strong architectural identity'. Therefore, the car park has taken on a semi-circular form, surrounded by oak trees on the curved side (yet to grow to their full height), and an arcade on the straight side which forms the entrance to the supermarket. The shop itself is standard, with an interior that might be found in any Sainsbury's between Dover and Durham – not fitted out by Dixon . Jones. The car park too is curiously orthodox in its layout – a grid of white lines on level tarmac with no shelter from wind or rain between shop and vehicle, except for disabled drivers.

The canopy and supermarket façade are undoubtedly the key features here. The canopy is made up of overlapping sails which take on different effects when viewed from different angles – from the motorway above they are sails, from the car park to the side they are like sections of a spine, and from underneath they make up the underbelly of a snake. Construction is of semi-translucent fabric stretched over an armature of steel structural members. The light screen below, which forms both the entrance and exit to the car park from one side and pedestrian access into the supermarket from the other, is made of perforated aluminium cladding panels with simple, clear labels showing bicycle, bus and information points. The arcade also provides a striking backdrop for the endless line of shopping

Devon

Jeremy Dixon . Edward Jones 1994

Devon

Jeremy Dixon . Edward Jones 1994

trolleys with their orange handles forming a coloured stripe along the arcade. A cafeteria has been introduced here and is shielded from the adjacent petrol garage by a black slate wall with minimally detailed window openings (no decorative surrounds) – similar to the wall to be found at The Henry Moore Institute in Leeds by the same architects (see page 46).

The project marks another step in the 1990s' reinterpretation of the 1980s' phenomenon of façadism. There is no attempt here to ape any particular style. Instead the architects have used the opportunity to create another kind of space and an event between the façade and the outside, when there is obviously no opportunity to deal with the building in its entirety.

STRUCTURAL ENGINEER Ernest Green Partnership
CLIENT: J Sainsbury's plc
SIZE building 26,400 square metres, sales area approximately 13,300 square metres, entire site 10.5 acres
CONTRACT VALUE £8.5 million
getting there take the A38 route into Plymouth from the east; Sainsbury's is on your left
ACCESS open

Devon

Jeremy Dixon . Edward Jones 1994

Devon

Jeremy Dixon . Edward Jones 1994

Western Morning News
Plymouth

Plymouth's sea-faring history is famous. The imagery used here at the *Western Morning News* offices and printworks is therefore not inappropriate, if a tad literal. The view of the building from the north is breathtaking (especially when the light is good). The ship cruises out of a grassy light-industrial plot, overlooking the suburbs of Plymouth. The visitor's introductory view (first entrance on left) is of sky and trees and the gentle curve of the 'tusk' columns leaning out from the building.

Walking past this elevation, you can see through the full-height glazed walls (as at Grimshaw's Financial Times Printworks in London's Docklands) into the print room – night is obviously the best time to see this, when the presses roll. The Planar glazing continues right round the perimeter of the building, hung between the tusks (each one made of two curved steel tubes with plate steel welded on either side) and a concrete column and flat-slab structure inside. The columns also support the bowed roof beams, pin-jointed beneath the tips of the tusks. The roof is clad in curved aluminium panels.

The plan of the building is split clearly into two. The stern accommodates the printroom into which is floated another steel and concrete frame lined with rubber which prevents low-frequency vibrations from the presses from reaching the 5000 square metres of office space in the prow. The two areas are further insulated from each other by a full-height fair-faced blockwork wall inside. The in-situ concrete tower is the main boardroom, rising 30 metres above ground level.

The development of the glazing system is an interesting feature of the building and one that has stumbled on the most pitfalls. The outward curve was based on the idea of a car windscreen where the tilt cuts out reflections whilst allowing maximum light in, without obscuring the view

Devon

Nicholas Grimshaw & Partners 1993

Devon

Nicholas Grimshaw & Partners 1993

with blinds. However this is not strictly true – sections of the editorial department in open-plan offices around the edges of the prow have suffered from severe glare on their VDUs and, at times, intense heat. The glass walls are now draped with canvas sails which can be unfurled by a manual cranking system – the architect justified the emergency measure by saying that 'it allows the occupants to have control over their own environment'. As a result the outward appearance is somewhat shambolic, with sails at full or half mast dripping inside the glass. The all-over-glazing concept has proved thoroughly unforgiving.

The other crucial disappointment is the treatment of the main entrance from the car park on the south. Staff and visitors enter the first floor via a drawbridge through automatic doors hanging from specially designed claw-brackets. Above the doors are two standard blow-heaters. After the intense consideration of materials and furniture elsewhere, this is a devastating compromise.

The Western Morning News is one of the most expressionistic projects in the country but, as the engineer Frank Newby has said: 'High tech is the use of tortured structure for decorative purposes'. There are limits to making attention-grabbing buildings – if the detailing is not refined enough to carry the technological concept through then the building is not wholly successful.

STRUCTURAL ENGINEER Ove Arup & Partners
SIZE 15,000 square metres
CONTRACT VALUE £15 million
GETTING THERE north out of the town centre on the A386, Derriford Business Park, 17 Brest Road, near the airport in the Derriford district
ACCESS very limited

Devon

Nicholas Grimshaw & Partners 1993

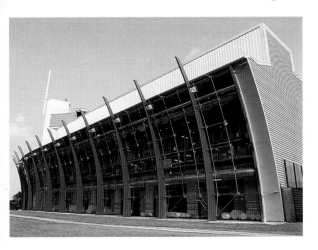

Nicholas Grimshaw & Partners 1993

Clovelly Visitors' Centre

This visitors' centre represents all that is most vacuous about an architectural genre which has mushroomed across the country over the last ten years. Clovelly is a working village – it is still full of real people with real jobs (mainly fishing) and real lives. It is also a major tourist attraction (another source of employment). With the tourist industry comes the problem of how to direct visitors through a place and make them leave feeling they have taken a bit of that place with them, while leaving it intact.

Victorian holidaymakers bought a souvenir (creating the postcard and seashell-encrusted picture frame industries). Today's tourists have been introduced to items such as the Bo-Peep tote bag (a bag which hangs over the side of your armchair, usually made in gaudy floral fabric, for your needlework, book or old fruitcake), and the canvas wellington-boot bag with oakleaf logo. These and many other items portray images of nature and of old-fashioned rural pastimes with uses adapted to a modern world. None of these items bears any relationship to the place visited.

The Clovelly visitors' centre is a perpetrator of this kind of enterprise. Your experience will begin by parking for free in front of the visitors' centre with its low-pitched slate roof surmounted by a decorative clock tower. Once inside, the full horror begins as you pay your entrance fee to be subjected to tables laden with books about 'How to Ice Birthday Cakes' and racks of misshapen lollipops, before entering the cafeteria. I arrived, needing sustenance for more site seeing, at 4 o'clock on an August afternoon and found one Cornish pasty, some dry scones, a cauldron of Heinz tomato soup, and a few sweating sandwiches.

The far end of the building is entirely glazed, showing off a panoramic view of the sea. Unfortunately, interior distractions, such as the Coca-Cola-sodden/crisp-encrusted carpet underfoot, the flimsy reproduction bentwood chairs and the steel-trussed roof festooned with plastic ivy in

Devon

Van Heyningen & Haward 1988

Devon

Van Heyningen & Haward 1988

hanging baskets, negate any attempt by the architect to make an informative and welcoming transition space from which to discover Clovelly village proper.

The village is a five-minute walk down a very steep cobbled path (it cannot be reached by car, although there is a special Land Rover service for those really in need). It is absolutely picturesque – a great pirate movie location. To my dismay I discovered a village post office selling books about the long history of the place, two little hotels overlooking the harbour and beyond, serving the ultimate in afternoon clotted-cream teas, and a woman in a hole in the cliff-face serving fresh crab sandwiches … if only I had known what was in store.

The arduous trek back up the hill takes about 15 minutes, but is thoroughly worth the effort, knowing that you can avoid going back into the visitors' centre by walking around the left-hand side of the building to the car park.

STRUCTURAL ENGINEER Price & Myers
CLIENT Clovelly Estate Company
SIZE approximately 1000 square metres
GETTING THERE on the B3237, off the A39 between Bideford and Bude
ACCESS open

Devon

Van Heyningen & Haward 1988

Devon

Van Heyningen & Haward 1988

Tate Gallery
St Ives

The Tate in St Ives was built to exhibit works by the St Ives school of artists (1930–75), including Barbara Hepworth, Naum Gabo, Roger Hilton, Ben Nicholson, Bernard Leach and Patrick Heron. These artists, and many more, were drawn here because of the rare and dramatic quality of light, the rich colours and geometric topography of the town and the surrounding rugged landscape with its unusual isolated rock features. The Barbara Hepworth Museum is close by and definitely worth visiting. There she describes 'the remarkable pagan landscape which lies between St Ives, Penzance and Land's End; a landscape which still has a very deep effect on me, developing all my ideas about the relationship of the human figure in landscape … essential quality of light in relation to sculpture which induced a new way of piercing forms to contain colour'.

The narrow, winding streets in St Ives are lined with tiny houses that climb the steep hill to surround the harbour and adjacent Porthmeor Beach. It is this asymmetrical street pattern and scale of building that has influenced the architects of the new gallery. The site is flanked by council houses on each side and bed and breakfasts behind.

The main entrance is at the lowest point of the site. Steps and ramps around the perimeter of a circular loggia lead you into a sheltered outdoor seating area before you enter the 'paying desk' corridor, moving swiftly through to the first attraction – a full-height stained-glass window by Patrick Heron, commissioned for this building. The stunning thing about the piece is that there are no leading lines. The coloured glass pieces are laminated onto a clear 15-mm-thick panel, a method devised by a window maker in Wiesbaden. Although the room is saturated in rich colours, the room itself remains cold.

Continuing on through another cold, anonymous space and up a stair,

Evans & Shalev 1991–93

Cornwall

Evans & Shalev 1991–93

you will begin to notice the twee bannister railings, already bound up with electrical tape in parts.

The five main galleries themselves are undoubtedly more inviting, based on the scale and proportions of some of the artists' studios, top lit and varying in shape and size according to the work on display. The curved ceramics gallery brings you back to the glass screen surrounding the front loggia and opens up a tremendous view of the ocean. The glass is wonderfully weather beaten, caked in a layer of salt spray, and lets in a cold white light. The crisp white restaurant is on the top floor and spills out on to open terraces with views of Porthmeor Beach, and down into the open central courtyard, shielded by a glass screen.

The architects wanted art, building, town and nature to unfold as one experience. The scale of the interior spaces achieves this, but the exterior is lacklustre. It must have something to do with the choice of white marble-chipping render which absorbs the light so that all the exterior surfaces appear flat. In a light mist the building is almost invisible.

St Ives' residents were sceptical about the need for a public gallery in a seaside town where a swimming baths might have been more useful for those wet summer holidays. However, the new Tate has made a significant impact, attracting thousands of visitors, enriching the tourist industry without resorting to white-knuckle-ride tactics.

STRUCTURAL ENGINEER Jenkins and Potter
CLIENT Cornwall County Council
CONTRACT VALUE £1,979,679.52
GETTING THERE site overlooks Porthmeor Beach, very close to the town centre on Beach Street. Pay car park up the hill on the same street
ACCESS open

Cornwall

Evans & Shalev 1991–93

Cornwall

Evans & Shalev 1991–93

Avon

**Bristol Development Corporation
Marketing Centre**
Bristol

This is a member of the 'little gem' school of architecture and a part of
the 1990s' epidemic of visitors' centres, flagships in city areas under redevelopment. What subsequently evolves in so many of these places are
shapes that we know all too well – multiplex cinemas and bowling alleys
in off-the-peg sheds. Here, however, the opportunity has been taken to
experiment with the technology of demountable buildings.

The 7-metre-high tower gives views of the redevelopment area from
a low point in the river valley. The surroundings are notbreathtaking but
the building itself is very inviting. The main body unwinds from the
central mast on legs which stand low in a shallow pool of water, like a
pavilion in a Japanese water garden. Access to the centre is via a wooden
gang-plank over the pool. Inside, the main space contains a predictable
display of visionary Cibachromes, top-lit from slits in the roof. The
central blue mast of the tower supports a fan of steel beams from which
the whole structure is hung. The two levels of main radial structural
members fold up for transportation. The floating decks are wooden
slatted and the first level is sheltered by a canvas canopy with the spiral
stair entwined round the mast. The structure has an elegant fragility (quite
wobbly on the top deck). It's exciting to see a building designed to be stabilised from the top down rather than from the bottom up, although here
the two seem to meet somewhere in the middle.

CONSULTING ENGINEER Whitby & Bird
GETTING THERE Avon Street is off the A4 spine road, opposite the Avon
& Somerset Constabulary
ACCESS open

Avon

Alec French Partnership 1994

Avon

Alec French Partnership 1994

The Arnolfini Arts Centre
Bristol

The Arnolfini Gallery was founded in the 1960s. Located in a converted Victorian dockside warehouse, it houses a video library, bookshop, bar and restaurant, performance space and galleries. The original conversion was one of the first examples in England of maintaining a façade while building a new structure within – a method which became popular in the 1980s. The location of the columns of the new structure bore no relation to the original shell (which could not be touched), so the architect, David Chipperfield, was forced to reorganise the circulation rather than take a fresh approach to the whole scheme.Detailing is rigidly executed, and there is a generally refined use of materials throughout – there is a clear definition between different surfaces and materials, including Portland stone, elm, ash, slate, marble and sycamore.

The bar/restaurant was designed in collaboration with the sculptor, Bruce McLean. Each element has been designed to determine how both customers and proprietors should use the space. A major sculptural work in its own right, the bar, a long terrazzo top on a steel base, dominates the room. The surfaces appear to have been drawn and painted directly into the space in big bold strokes.

Seating is raised on a plinth to gain a view through the windows. The long refectory tables and bench seating can accommodate large group meetings and provide a workman-like atmosphere. Even the thin, minimal beer pumps were designed as part of the total concept.

GETTING THERE south of the centre of town, where Wapping Road meets Prince Street, next to the Information Centre
ACCESS galleries open Monday to Saturday 10.00– 19.00, Sunday 12.00– 18.00; bar open Monday to Saturday 10.00–23.00, Sunday 12.30–22.30

Avon

David Chipperfield Architects 1987

Avon

David Chipperfield Architects 1987

Biodrier
Avonmouth

This building houses Britain's first Biodrier, a mechanical device which dries, sieves and mills sewage, producing Biograin, a rich, dry and odourless fertiliser. Methane, a by-product, is filtered and recycled, 70 per cent of the heat is recycled and the liquid by-product is bottled and used in the chemical industry. Why is this all happening? Because 30 million tonnes of sewage is produced in the UK every year. Before the plant was built, in the Bristol area 70 per cent of the stuff was spread on the land and the rest was dumped in the ocean. An EC directive to be enforced by 1998 seeks alternatives to dumping, with preference given to incineration, landfill or recycling. The difficulty with the first two is the volume of methane produced. Recycling addresses the use of all the elements.

The plant is housed in a tall hanger-like shed with a boldly curved roof (compare the Power Station, Eye, page 190). The structure is steel on a brick plinth, clad in a double layer of silver aluminium panels. The roof is elevated on struts to allow space for ventilation louvres at clerestory level. The proportions are generous and the roof looks as if it might take flight at any minute. It hovers in the flat landscape like an enormous beetle, alongside the industrial dinosaurs grazing in the bleak docklands.

STRUCTURAL ENGINEER Whicheloe Macfarlane
GETTING THERE from Bristol, take the A4 to Avonmouth, follow the river under Clifton Suspension Bridge. At the roundabout follow signs left to centre of Avonmouth, on St Andrews Road. A mile past the second roundabout there are some traffic lights; turn right on to Kings Western Lane (signs to Britannia Zinc). Half a mile down the lane there is a turning on your left and you will see the building on the horizon
ACCESS by appointment only; call Wessex Water

Avon

Whicheloe Macfarlane 1994

Whicheloe Macfarlane 1994

Building 6 East, Bath University

This is the School of Architecture and Building Engineering, and forms a new entrance to the university campus from the east side. This is also an opportunity to see the recent work of an architectural partnership who's thinking has been both influential and revolutionary since the 1950s. The building has a rawness which suggests that it is a 'teaching building', i.e. each detail is a lesson in dealing with either volume, quality of light, sound, materials or services. No two rooms are the same but they share all the same components.

The staircase running up the north side of the building is the strategic element which leads you into the pedestrianised campus. At this level there are seminar rooms, exhibition spaces, lecture theatres and offices, with studios above where there is the benefit of more natural light. All the components of construction are visible throughout-- the post-and-slab concrete frame with exterior stone in-fill walls and off-the-peg aluminium window frames, fair-faced concrete columns, lintels and lift and stair shaft. Internal walls are painted plaster, floors are painted screed, all pipework and electrical conduit is exposed, different species of wood are used for diffferent parts of the door frames to show clearly the way that they have been constructed.

The project is an on-going experiment into how we colonise and construct a space, given that the space is already awkward, rather than taking the abstract approach of trying to rationalise a white cube.

STRUCTURAL ENGINEER Harris Sutherland
CLIENT University of Bath
GETTING THERE the Badgerline bus route takes you from the centre of town to the door
ACCESS limited

Avon

Alison and Peter Smithson 1988

Avon

Alison and Peter Smithson 1988

Hampshire

Farnborough Grange Junior School
Farnborough

There is an unusual atmosphere here. The children are riotous, the teachers are shouting and the building fabric is run down. This does not fit into the pattern of other Hampshire schools where building and users seem to be in harmony.

Several factors perhaps contribute to the discord. The plan is a trefoil shape. Three arms protrude from a central lookout tower with the staff-room at the top (reminiscent of a prison guard's lookout). Two south-facing arms accommodate cellular classrooms which feed off north-facing corridors and meet in the middle at the resource centre. The corridors are dark and cramped and full of coats, gym bags and football boots. The classrooms, although glazed on the south side and opening onto a garden area, are still sealed units from the inside – the space does not have the relaxed, free plan of other schools. The third arm accommodates the offices, kitchens, changing rooms and sports hall at the end. This and the north-facing (corridor) walls of the other two arms are all faced in insulated brick. They form the exterior elevations surrounding the break-time play areas – all hard surfaces with few windows, the children sit on the concrete entrance courtyard, patrolled by dinner ladies in pink overalls, to eat their packed lunches.

The trefoil plan lacks the communal space which is so generous at other Hampshire schools. The arterial routes lead in one direction, to the centre, but the central space is cramped.

A new dimension was added to the conventional clerestory in the roof. The roofs are made up of a double curve. The lower concave surface reflects high summer sun into the protruding lip of the counter curve of the higher roof section which bounces the light through the clerestory on to the ceiling inside. The low winter sun filters directly through the clere-

Edward Cullinan Architects 1991

Hampshire

Edward Cullinan Architects 1991

story which can be opened for natural ventilation. Exterior plywood cladding on the south-facing classrooms is suffering from vandalism. The surrounding landscape is the same as the suburban landscape beyond the school boundary.

Many of the fundamental characteristics of the Hampshire school programme have been addressed but without due consideration to the scale and organisation of the building in relation to its users, and without belief in the children's ability to discipline themselves – the rules have been laid down in the hierarchy of the spaces.

STRUCTURAL ENGINEER YRM Anthony Hunt Associates
CLIENT Hampshire Education Department
SIZE 1100 square metres
CONTRACT VALUE £1 million
GETTING THERE on Cherrywood Road off Renway, near Farnborough Football Club
ACCESS telephone the secretary first and announce yourself on arrival

Edward Cullinan Architects 1991

Hampshire

Edward Cullinan Architects 1991

Park Hill Primary School
Aldershot

The site is in the middle of a 1930s' housing estate on the outskirts of Aldershot. The school is one of the latest in the county's list of successful projects, injecting youthful vitality into a sleepy suburb. The plan follows the 'street' (Queen's Inclosure and, more loosely, Woodlea) as opposed to the 'spiral' pattern (Stoke Park Infants). The spaces are arranged in a linear fashion with the sports hall at the head, the classrooms forming the body and the music room at the tail end.

The approach to the school is from the west. A wide path leads to the fortress-like brick, drum-shaped hall lit internally by a clerestory band beneath a shallow conical roof. The path continues up a gradual slope to the south side of the building which stretches along side it. Children and parents are led by patterns painted on the ground in the form of games – hopscotch, snakes and ladders – craftily pointing them in the direction of their classrooms as they arrive in the morning. Classrooms line the south side of the street, each one defined by its mono-pitched roof emphasising the organic form of the plan (inspired by Van Eyck's Sonsbeck Sculpture Pavilion in Arnhem, according to the architect). The barriers between parent, teacher and pupil are eliminated here as they all congregate in the mornings in the garden areas directly outside each classroom. Wooden fences divide the gardens, give shelter from the wind and perform an essential and traditional function as 'the sociable garden fence' – a device for the exchange of gossip.

The roof pitches open towards the east so that the inside of each classroom is filled with natural light and stripes of sunlight cross the street area like zebra crossings (the most successful natural-light admitting device that I seen have so far in the Hampshire school series). Exposed roof supports are made from twice-sawn timber with a natural seal

Hampshire County Council Architects Department 1994

Hampshire County Council Architects Department 1994

exuding a wonderful woody smell rather than the usual odour of school dinners and old plimsolls. The trusses and full-width beams span the entire width of the street and classrooms resting on shallow brick piers (with sturdy brick diaphragm walls between) and extend outside to form deep eaves that reveal the layered structure of the ceiling. Inside it is insulated, the eaves showing the skeletal form of the rafters and trusses supporting Redland tiles. Zinc funnels protruding from the base of each monopitch are attached to yellow downpipes for drainage.

Classrooms are separated from the street by glazed walls which act as a sound baffle whilst maintaining the openness of the plan. This allows overall supervision at all times by teachers, and pupils can see each other's work quite freely. Again, there is a physical divide between each classroom, white-painted brick enclosures protruding into the street space to form changing booths and miniature kitchen areas.

The arrangement at Park Hill promotes cooperation between all its users and the loose definition of inside and outside provides enough space (and in wet weather, the sensation of enough space) to cope with the unflagging effervescence of small children.

PROJECT ARCHITECT Joe Collins
STRUCTURAL ENGINEER Dave Shaw
CLIENT Hampshire Education Department
CONTRACT VALUE £600 per square metre
GETTING THERE off the Lower Farnham Road (A324), on the west (Guildford) side of Aldershot. Turn right before meeting the main Ash/Guildford Road (A323) on to Gloucester Road
ACCESS telephone the secretary first and announce yourself on arrival

Hampshire

Hampshire County Council Architects Department 1994

Hampshire County Council Architects Department 1994

Woodlea Primary School
Bordon

The RIBA's 'Building of the Year 1994', this is the latest in a line of distinguished Hampshire schools. As Frank Duffy said at the awards ceremony: 'The team and architectural tradition … epitomise the cumulative, long-term and totally magical benefits of creative architects simultaneously working with their clients to articulate their requirements as well as capturing their clients' imagination with humane architectural invention'. The form, plan and substance of Woodlea originate in the landscape and are a continuation of the 'Learning through Landscape' movement, initiated by the council and now established as a trust which aims to promote the development, appreciation and use as a learning resource of the neglected landscape surrounding schools and other buildings.

On the edge of a housing estate, the site is a piece of ancient oak, birch and pine woodland sloping away from Iron-Age earthworks. The architects have used the contours of the land to determine the curved plan of the school, causing minimum disruption to the landscape. The organisation of the plan follows that of other Hampshire schools: a central arterial route and communal space from which classrooms, administration and the main hall branch out. Here the change in levels logically helped to determine the layout. The main entrance, administration, library and central resource are on the middle level, with ramps up to the hall, music and drama room and changing rooms, and ramp and steps down towards teaching areas, the exterior decking and a cocooned view through an opening in the woods down to the playing field beyond.

This inward-facing side is made from soft materials: a Douglas fir timber frame with laminated beams, boarded ceilings and cedar shingle roofs. Classrooms have encaustic-tiled floors, each designed by a different artist. Outward facing walls, that is, the entrance façades and the eleva-

Hampshire County Council Architects Department 1993

Hampshire

Hampshire County Council Architects Department 1993

tions skirting the hall, use harder materials such as rough stock brick, with terracotta tiles on the roofs. Internal light is mainly diffused and refracted natural light admitted through clerestory windows and rooflights.

The hall takes on an anatomical form, like the inside of a whale's stomach. It is encased in a series of Glu-lam beam ribs which grow from the floor in a huge arch. The natural shapes take away all of the gloom associated with school halls, without resorting to patronising primary colours and simplistic geometric shapes.

This building shows a series of straightforward, very well executed details, put together simply; small buildings growing up organically around the higher main hall. Internal and external spaces flow together with wooden decking terraces acting as intermediate spaces. It is like a rabbit warren, in scale with the children, but without being claustrophobic due to the penetration of natural light, frequent transitions between levels and inside and outside spaces, and a close affinity with its naturally beautiful site.

The school is attended by 245 children between 5 and 11 years old. The atmosphere is remarkable – simultaneous excitement and tranquillity. There are spaces in which to run around freely and small corners in which to curl up on your own. The architects wanted to create a 'total learning environment' and seem to have succeeded.

PROJECT ARCHITECT Joe Collins
CLIENT Hampshire Education Department
GETTING THERE Bordon is off the A325, south of Farnham, 4 miles along the Bordon road to the roundabout with a garage. Turn left and Athle Road is the second on the right
ACCESS telephone the secretary first and announce yourself on arrival

Hampshire

Hampshire County Council Architects Department 1993

Hampshire County Council Architects Department 1993

Liss Junior School

A major factor in the success of the Hampshire schools programme is the imaginative siting of the buildings – the landscape is always considered to be an important extension of the building. Liss is no exception, set against a hillside looking over the infants school directly below, towards beautiful rolling hills to the south and resting against a steep grassy bank behind. It was built on the potential profits of the sale of the land where the old Victorian school (now boarded up) still stands in the village. A very close client/architect relationship helped to experiment and develop another phase in the evolution of the Hampshire school ideology.

From the outside the building looks unusually sanitary, like a small hospital – a sweeping drive, gleaming white walls, with a deep recessed corner porch supported by a slender column, tall bay windows facing south, a gently saw-toothed roofline with gutters running into minimal pebble troughs. The roof top is covered in grass so that the building disappears into the landscape when viewed from the houses further up the hill.

Inside, a very sophisticated environment has emerged. A central winding blue carpet flows up the hill, with teaching areas on the south side and the hall, lavatories and some enclosed teaching spaces on the north. Rooflights fill the entire lofty space with natural light which reflects off the bright white interior walls – there is not a natural timber rafter to be seen, no low cosy corners. You feel like you are on top of the world, nearly touching the sky (large, spherical white paper lampshades fill the river/street area like billowing clouds). The whole space can be viewed from the staff balcony above the reception area during indoor playtimes.

The teaching areas, with the youngest children at the bottom of the hill and the eldest at the top next to the playground, are separated from each other by full-height partition walls but there is no barrier between the classrooms and the street. Inevitably, noise does travel. This can be

Hampshire

Hampshire County Council Architects Department 1994

most distracting but it puts tremendous pressure on the children to be disciplined and to learn to respect each other's space and privacy. They are all remarkably well behaved. When I visited the school a child was having a violin lesson in one of the teaching areas; the noise was almost too much to bear, although, as the headteacher explained, this was an opportunity for the other children to do their noisier lessons too, like woodwork.

The quality of the space has begun to determine the way that the children use it. All of the plywood furniture was designed specially for the school by a Swedish firm, with the assistance of interior designer Anne Humphrey, and provided a lesson in ergonomics for children who were directly involved in testing the prototypes. The hall on the north side is completely sound-proofed but the only problem so far has been the access to it, which at present is either from the outside (no good during wet weather) or through reception, which is too distracting. This is currently being reassessed.

PROJECT ARCHITECT Ian Templeton
STRUCTURAL ENGINEER Brian Veck
CLIENT Hampshire Education Department
SIZE 1249 square metres
GETTING THERE Liss is signposted off the A3 north of Petersfield, on the B3006. The school is on the north side of the village
ACCESS telephone the secretary first then announce yourself on arrival

Hampshire

Hampshire

Hampshire County Council Architects Department 1994

Queen's Inclosure Middle School
Cowplain, Waterlooville

David Moriss, project architect, saw no point in re-inventing the wheel when he took on the design of this school. Queen's Inclosure owes much to Hopkins' Velmead Infants School (see page 304) and has learnt from many of its mistakes. The architect's idea behind the brief was the 'need to look at middle school education afresh, as a termination of primary education. This was also in tune with the national curriculum, the emphasis being on learning and by seeing what others are doing.'

The basic plan is a central street with teaching areas on one side and administration and sports hall on the other, with floating quiet rooms in the middle. However, here the orientation of the building is the opposite to Velmead, with classrooms facing north, views across the Forest of Bere and exterior teaching areas, the offices on the south side looking out over a meadow and the main lavender-lined entrance walk and meadow. Inside, the isolated pods face on to the street so that they can also be used as group teaching spaces for cooking and crafts. Turning them round (they face towards the classrooms at Velmead) helps to separate them acoustically from the noisier class spaces. Greater acoustic separation between the classes has been achieved by inserting glass screens, although pupils are still free to wander between spaces.

The roof profile has been successfully altered, a central rooflight spine like Velmead, but with barrel vaulting either side made of curved profiled-metal roof-sheeting. This device not only enhances the natural light which flows in from the glazed north and south elevations but also makes the interior feel considerably more spacious – there is limitless horizon in all directions. At Velmead the sloping roof line seems to depress the natural light. The south elevation has an overhang of semi-parabolic veins to shade the offices, but budget cuts meant that reflector veins to bounce

Hampshire County Council Architects Department 1990

Hampshire

Hampshire County Council Architects Department 1990

more light inside could not be added to the north side.

The free plan works as the most flexible plan gives flexibility – it copes with the increasing number of pupils at the school which was originally designed for 260 children but now has nearly 400. The school succeeds as a social exercise, producing confident children, used to being confronted by adults and children of different ages as they roam around. There have been good results with 'bad-behaviour cases' because so much of the teaching is based on trust – children are encouraged to work alone or in groups with their friends, to use the resources provided rather than relying on teachers to spoon feed information. From the teaching point of view, the free plan has done away with 'lazy-teacher syndrome'; it demands an active contribution.

Educational arguments are often polarised – radical versus traditional – but what really happens day to day lies somewhere in between. This school building allows that to happen.

STRUCTURAL ENGINEER R J Watkinson and Partners
CLIENT Hampshire Education Department
SIZE 1386 square metres
CONTRACT VALUE £1,042,211
GETTING THERE from the north, take the A3 south to Cowplain over the A3(M) bypass, through Cowplain, Waitrose supermarket on right, woodland on left, left on to Highfield Avenue; Cornelius Drive is the second left by the shops
ACCESS telephone the secretary first and announce yourself on arrival

Hampshire

Hampshire County Council Architects Department 1990

Hampshire

Hampshire County Council Architects Department 1990

Stoke Park Infants School
Bishopstoke

The school's teepee roof protrudes from a dip in the ground, created by banking up soil all round the building as a protective shield. Influenced by Burnham Copse Infant School at Tadley, a spiral plan unwinds in layers with the hall at the centre underneath the apex of the roof. The ceiling reveals Glu-lam timber rafters with a vertical beam and steel spoke-wheel bracing arrangement that doubles as a lighting rig. A skylight at the top contains an openable central vent. Immediately surrounding the hall are staff offices and a mezzanine band of shared space overlooking the centre from which steps branch off anti-clockwise, leading into nine split-level south-facing classrooms.

From the outside the multi-pitched roof, finished with bands of zinc, cedar shingles and glazing indicate how the spaces are defined internally. It unwinds like a stiffly draped skirt flaring up at the edges to create shallow eaves.

The plan is complex to describe because of its many interior levels but once actually inside the building the circulation seems logical and visibility between the spaces is clear. The combination of small home spaces and large communal spaces introduce a small child to a broader social structure.

PROJECT ARCHITECT Stephen Harte
STRUCTURAL ENGINEER Buro Happold
CLIENT Hampshire Education Department
CONTRACT VALUE £1.1 million
GETTING THERE halfway between Eastleigh and Fairoaks on the B3037, turn left on to Abbotsbury Road
ACCESS telephone the secretary first and announce yourself on arrival

Hampshire

Hampshire County Council Architects Department 1989

Hampshire County Council Architects Department 1989

Velmead Infants School
Fleet

Michael Hopkins & Partners were commissioned by Hampshire County Council in 1984 to design this school; Colin Stansfield-Smith was keen for them to apply their Teflon-coated-fabric technology which seemed to express a free-flowing internal plan. The scheme – translucent fabric roof with a rectangular glazed box beneath – was rejected by the Education Committee apparently because of the relatively short life of the fabric (20–25 years), although initially it would have been considerably cheaper than a conventional roof. The roof structure eventually employed – a sloping pitch with a central spine ridge, is in the Hampshire school tradition and forms a glass and steel pavilion. It is set between a suburban pinewood and boggy marshland.

The plan has nine open class 'bases' lining the south side and boxed-in cellular spaces for administration, the main entrance and the main hall on the north side. The quiet areas, or 'pods', float freely either side of a central street but face on to the class areas. This seems to create a corridor effect in the street, rather than a communal space for group work. The central skylight ridge also emphasises the linearity of the building, again diminishing the sense of distance and space (a factor that the membrane roof would have addressed more appropriately). The height overall is determined by the 3.2-metre wall height necessary for the sports hall at the north-west corner of the plan. This means that the whole space becomes uniform, which again goes against the Hampshire grain. On the exterior, each class base with external play area is defined by a structural bay and sunshade (unfortunately the sunshades don't keep the rain off). These architect-versus-user problems seem to be a direct result of the initial compromise on the roof structure.

Instead, the architect's expression and expertise have been focused on

Michael Hopkins & Partners 1987

Hampshire

Michael Hopkins & Partners 1987

the structural details such as the 'dumbbell' column (it looks like a dumbbell in plan), the internal column doubles as a rain water pipe, leaving the external column to appear as slim structure. Another invisible trick is in the roof where three-quarters of the rafters' depth is lost behind acoustic and thermal insulated decking. At the eaves the rafters appear to float and there is no clash between metal roof deck and perimeter frame with glass walls. The perimeter glazing is not particularly energy efficient but the architect justifies it by pointing out the deep plan and the need for natural light to infiltrate all areas of the building – additional artificial lighting in the class areas seems muted and ineffectual.

Despite some conflict between an architect's expectation of the architecture and the users' experience, the head of the school has been delighted with the way the building works. Due to retire this year, she will be devastated to leave. She explained that there is a traditional-style school down the road: 'This is for *Telegraph* readers where the parents say they like the school. At Velmead we attract the *Independent* and *Guardian* readers where the children say they like the school.'

STRUCTURAL ENGINEER Buro Happold
CLIENT Hampshire County Council
CONTRACT VALUE £556,199 (£60,362 for external works)
GETTING THERE leave the M3 at junction 4A, follow signs to Fleet. Pass Fleet station on the left, and turn left at the next set of traffic lights on to King's Road. At the next lights (approximately 1 mile) go straight on, over a canal bridge, and take a right on to Velmead Road. The school is on the left-hand side of the road
ACCESS telephone the secretary first and announce yourself on arrival

Hampshire

Michael Hopkins & Partners 1987

Michael Hopkins & Partners 1987

County Records Office
Winchester

Hampshire County Council isn't just good at designing schools but can tackle other building types with equal gusto. The County Records Office is a landmark building, marking a new gateway into Winchester in a rather worn-out corner which seems to have slipped through the hands of the conservationists who have a firm grip on the rest of the city. Commissioned by Freddie Emery-Wallis (the head of the County Council who encouraged the school-building programme) to replace the previous repository (a converted Victorian church), the building houses certificates of births, deaths and marriages, parish registers, and historical documents, such as the love letters of Jane Austen.

The structure has three distinctive elements: brick base, glass pavilion, roof. From different sides it takes on different characters. Sited on a steep slope, the base is a brick wedge which slots into the hillside, reminiscent of an Italian Renaissance palazzo – deep stone or brick walls with small window openings defined by smooth stone architraves.

From the bottom of the hill the perspective seems to be tremendously exaggerated, making the first impression all the more imposing. At this base point there are four floors (including a very high lower ground floor), but when you get to the entrance further up the hill there are only three floors; the brick has diminished and the building becomes a south-west-facing glass and steel pavilion.

The pavilion's main elevation is made up of diagonally stepped terraces and balconies which overlook a small grassy courtyard and a short-cut from the station to the city centre. A shallow pebbled Japanese stream runs between the ground floor and the lawn, creating a tranquil atmosphere in the garden, like an inner courtyard. Inside, the lower ground floor (secure area enclosed by brick) houses the bookstore and services, the

Hampshire

Hampshire County Council Architects Department 1993

Hampshire County Council Architects Department 1993

ground floor is the entrance, with a triangular public search/reading room to the left and repository on the right, the first floor is a continuation of the repository and a void over the double-height space of the search room; the top floor houses a cinema, all of the office space and conservation rooms. Spaces are small because of the carefully controlled environmental conditions for the documents (stored on 8 miles of shelving) but the top floor maintains the loftiness of the space; the steep saw-tooth roofline creates more openings for natural light to fill the room than a series of rooflights might. The ground, first and second floors are also surrounded by glass walls which help to achieve a sense of openness and connection with the outside even if the internal arrangement is partitioned.

The third element, the striking saw-tooth roofline, seems to float independently above the glass, perhaps because it extends beyond the glass walls to create deep eaves over balconies, so the proportions again seem exaggerated.

It has been reported that Mike Hancock, successor to Emery-Wallis, has said that he is 'diametrically opposed' to the policies of his predecessor and unsympathetic to the strong position of the county's department of progressive architects. Concerned with conservation and restoration of historic buildings, he sees no need for so much new building. Conservation, restoration and progressive movement should each know when it is appropriate to open the door for the other.

STRUCTURAL ENGINEER R J Watkinson and Partners
CLIENT Hampshire County Council
GETTING THERE at the junction off Sussex Street, City Road, Andover Road and Stockbridge Road, near the railway station
ACCESS by appointment only

Hampshire

Hampshire County Council Architects Department 1993

Hampshire

Hampshire County Council Architects Department 1993

Kent, Sussex, Surrey

Channel Tunnel UK Passenger Terminal
Folkestone

The brief for one of this century's major building and engineering projects encompassed the overall site layout, earthworks, infrastructure, landscape, planning and designing of the buildings, interiors, signing and acoustics – more like designing a small town than a road/rail interchange. Traffic has to move quickly, safely and efficiently from the M20 through frontier controls and on to the shuttles. At the same time, the impact of the terminal on the neighbouring community has been addressed.

Speculative tunnelling began way back in 1882 but was soon halted by the British War Office. As air-warfare capabilities increased between the World Wars, the strategic significance of the Channel lessened and trade became the priority. Boring began again in the mid 1970s, this attempt being halted by recession. But along came the 1980s' boom and agreement between France and Britain to build the tunnel was reached in 1986. Eurotunnel, as the new company was to be called, won Royal Assent to build the link in return for the right to operate it for 55 years from 1987.

Rail passengers travel directly from London's Waterloo Railway Terminal (by Nicholas Grimshaw & Partners) and remain on the train until they reach Paris or Brussels three hours later. At some point in the future St Pancras Station is intended to become the main London terminal because of its direct interchange link with the north of Britain – why this was not considered before the Waterloo Terminal was built is anyone's guess. Car passengers will drive to Folkestone and board enclosed carriages, remaining in their cars for the hour-long journey.

The layout of the Folkestone site was developed to accommodate many different types and sizes of structures. The architects describe the plan vaguely as 'related grids providing a hidden basis for coordinating roads,

Kent

Kent

BDP 1994

structures, landscape and signs.' The primary elements on the site that are encompassed within the first imaginary grid are the arrival loop tunnel, the tourist causeway and bridges leading to the platforms and the rail tracks and tunnel opening, all designed so that there is no need for passengers to leave their cars. Then there are the public buildings which are designed as pavilions to punctuate the route. This is clear from an aerial view but on the ground the journey around the site is through a jungle of pylons, signs and vast expanses of tarmac.

The passenger amenity building at the centre of the site lies low in the landscape and has a lightweight fabric-covered tensile roof to act as a beacon for passengers. The round window in the top and surrounding clerestory windows just beneath the skirt of the roof allow changing light to fill a central concourse inside. At night, the translucency of the fabric creates a glow like a lighthouse. At the highest point of the site is the control centre, essentially road and rail traffic control – it is intended to be a distinctive visual marker in the tradition of air-traffic-control towers, although it lacks any of the elegance of buildings in a similar genre in the world of aviation.

The cost of the French and British terminals together was £540 million – one sixteenth of the total project cost.

The 50-km tunnel is actually three tunnels, two 7.6-metre-diameter running tunnels for the trains and one 4.8-metre-diameter service tunnel in the middle with cross-over points in between, all reaching a depth of 127 metres below sea level. Full-face tunnel-boring machines drove through the earth whilst other machines erected pre-cast-concrete segments behind to form a lining that could withstand twice the pressure imposed upon a nuclear power-station vessel. The first breakthrough occurred on 22 May 1991 and the final one on 28 June 1991 whereupon

Kent

Kent

BDP 1994

the British machines were buried in concrete below the tunnel bore. Trains run at approximately 130 km per hour through the tunnel and are capable of accumulating a 50° Celsius rise in temperature. To cool the tunnels, hair-pin-shaped chilled-water circuits run halfway down the tunnels served by land-based chillers. Fire-hydrant equipment is placed every 125 metres in the running tunnels with a supplementary vent system to extract smoke.

The tunneling project is a major engineering feat. The terminal is the first bewildering step of your journey. On an adjacent site, the Eurotunnel exhibition describes the history of the project and shows tunnelling equipment.

ARCHITECT, CIVIL, TRAFFIC, STRUCTURAL, MECHANICAL AND ELECTRICAL ENGINEER, ACOUSTICIAN, LANDSCAPE ARCHITECT, INTERIOR DESIGNER, PRODUCT DESIGNER GRAPHIC DESIGNER, QUANTITY SURVEYOR, PROJECT PLANNER BDP
CONTRACTOR Transmanche Link, a British and French consortium
CLIENT Eurotunnel
SIZE 142 hectares (350 acres), one third the size of its French counterpart
CONTRACT VALUE £10 billion
GETTING THERE the Eurotunnel Exhibition Centre is off junction 12 on the M20 – follow signs
ACCESS scheduled service only on four-minute bus tour, hourly from 10.30 to 15.30 (in the summer to 16.30)

Kent

BDP 1994

Kent

BDP 1994

Chaucer College, University of Kent
Canterbury

There is something distinctly oriental about this outcrop of buildings. The flavour comes from the fact that the college, sponsored by a wealthy Japanese patron, has been designed to accommodate 200 visiting Japanese students in an environment which would make them feel at home.

The entrance transports you immediately to Japan – a two-storey courtyard surrounded by library and classrooms on the north and west sides and a double-height dining hall on the south-east side. The outdoor room is tranquil and cloistered the air filled with the rich smell of the covered timber walkway that surrounds you. The horizontal balustrading is a particularly Far Eastern influence, emphasising the safe, all-encompassing nature of the courtyard. Out on the other side a view of the dining hall can be seen clearly in profile and, behind you, the rural Kentish setting. The dining hall is set on a brick base with Planar glazing above which meets the exaggerated outline of the roof – the two Roman-tiled slopes dip towards one another on Glu-lam beams but do not meet at the top. There is a gap at the apex forming a U-shaped channel and doubling up as an inverted clerestory. Natural light spills in through this channel on to the exposed roof trusses inside. In order to achieve the internal full-height space and reduce lateral stresses, a lattice of white steel tie-bars converge on steel balls suspended between the beams. The effect is ungainly when compared to the softness of the wood and the theatricality of the roofs.

Housed parallel to this but further down the hill is the students' common room and lecture theatre based very much on the same theme. The two- or three-storey residential blocks are to the south and east of the communal blocks and oriented towards the south, following the slope of the hill and overlooking the town. Each group of rooms is off a central

Kent

HKPA 1992

staircase, in the Oxbridge tradition, with a shared kitchen/common room. The roof pattern is the same, but there are no clerestory windows in the roof channels which transforms this feature into giant guttering, protruding on to the surrounding landscaped gardens.

The buildings move away from the bleak tradition of the rest of the University of Kent campus, which is something to be thankful for. But Chaucer College has also been sited away from the main campus which is enough to make any foreign student feel even more of an outsider. Apparently rooms have been taken up within the college by British students as the Japanese quota could not be filled – if it had been it might have had a more interesting effect on the community.

STRUCTURAL ENGINEER F J Samuely & Partners
CLIENT Shumi Gakuen, Japan
SIZE 7000 square metres
CONTRACT VALUE £8.5 million
GETTING THERE follow signs north on the A290 from the centre of the town to 'the university' up the hill overlooking the whole town. Chaucer College is also signposted
ACCESS announce yourself; it is easier to wander around during term time

Kent

HKPA 1992

J Sainsbury's Supermarket
Canterbury

Sainsbury's supermarket buildings have always stood out from the rest of the barnyard crowd. Increasingly they are gaining a reputation for stores which look a little out of the ordinary. Particularly in the last few years, several shops spead throughout the country have been built to standard requirements, but are adorned with frontages designed by a variety of distinguished architects – Nicholas Grimshaw in north London, Terry Farrell in Harlow, Lifschutz Davison in Coventry and Jeremy Dixon . Edward Jones in Plymouth. Instead of visiting an anonymous hangar and making our way through its aisles like a ball-bearing in a pinball machine, to be ejected violently into the car park at the end, there are now transition points. In Coventry and at Plymouth the transitional point is the façade, behind which lies a standard supermarket. The frontages in no way extend the use of or suggest an easier way to move from shop to car, neither do they offer additional services (there is an in-store café at Plymouth) such as dry cleaning or photocopying. The frontage serves as a beacon.

Ten years ago, in Canterbury, the entire shed was addressed by the guest architect (as at the Camden store). The glazed concrete blockwork envelope lies low beneath a mast-and-cable suspended structure, enabling a structure-free interior (of the standard variety). The plan is in three blocks: sales area, storage area and receiving area. Offices and staff rooms are in separate accommodation. The thin roof plane is supported from above by paired masts placed 3 metres apart. The spaces in between accommodate the service zone (with air-handling eqipment, etc.). The extension of the masts 1.5 metres above the tiles has no structural justification – it is more a tenuous statement on the part of the architect to echo the pinnacles of the cathedral in the distance, or, more tangibly, to

Kent

Ahrends Burton Koralek 1984

Kent

Ahrends Burton Koralek 1984

reduce the bulk of the building in the landscape. There is a suspended fabric canopy along the south-west-facing glazed elevation which defines a route for the pedestrian customers, extending around to the corner entrance which is defined by its own mast.

What makes these Sainsbury's schemes distinctive is that the context inspires expressive structures (particularly roofs) without local themes being adopted literally – they are part of the edge- of-town experience.

STRUCTURAL ENGINEER Anthony Hunt & Partners/Ernest Green Partnership
CLIENT J Sainsbury plc
SIZE approximately 3750 square metres
GETTING THERE Kingsmead Road, Canterbury
ACCESS open

Kent

Ahrends Burton Koralek 1984

Kent

Ahrends Burton Koralek 1984

Sussex Stand, Goodwood Racecourse

Arup Associates were commissioned in 1987 to upgrade the racecourse bringing it up to modern standards, and to clear away the jumble of Portakabins that were strewn around the stands. The plan included the new stand, next to the ten-year-old concrete stand by Howard Lobb and Jan Brabowski which casts a grim shadow over the ground and the spectators. The winning post was moved 50 metres, shifting the centre of gravity of the course and bringing it in line with the new views from the west-facing grandstand.

The stand's obvious attraction is the snow-white peaked fabric roof – a visual delight, a landmark, lightweight and structurally economical. It is three bays wide, the primary structure using rods as opposed to cables (as used at the Mound Stand at Lord's Cricket Ground, London, by Michael Hopkins, also engineered by Ove Arup). Wind pressures here are estimated to be double those in central London and the site is exposed on top of a hill, but the stresses are also great because the structure is asymmetrical – maximum force is exerted on the lifting ring around each peak where the membrane is reinforced with another layer of fabric. Although the peaks appears to be made of an extruded stretchy material, the shapes are, in fact, cut to a precise pattern. There is relatively little give in the reinforced polyester PVC material, hoisted into place and then tensioned with cables attached to the steel booms underneath and at the back of the stand, and by cables at the front. Polyester PVC was chosen because it was half the cost of Teflon-coated glassfibre although its life expectancy is also about half – approximately fifteen years.

The internal hierarchy of floors has been altered to allow the paying public to have the best views from the floating top tier under the canopy. The upmarket entertainment suites are at ground level, a concrete and brick-clad block where eating, drinking and socialising are the priority.

Arup Associates 1990

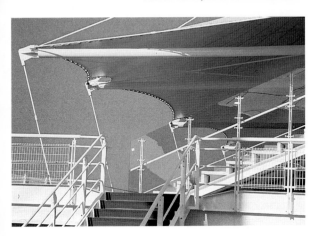

West Sussex

Arup Associates 1990

Arup Associates have a very practical approach towards building and they are becoming increasingly involved in the construction of stadiums and leisure facilities in the 1990s. As this stand is only used for seventeen days in the summer they might have developed the programme for the underbelly of the building, affording a little more glamour. The attention to the roof alone does not make a complete building, especially when compared to a well-developed project such as the Mound Stand.

West Sussex

STRUCTURAL ENGINEER Arup Associates/Ove Arup & Partners
CLIENT Goodwood Racecourse
GETTING THERE take the A286 north out of Chichester, a right-hand turn is signposted to East Lavant and Goodwood beyond
ACCESS open during the season in summer

Arup Associates 1990

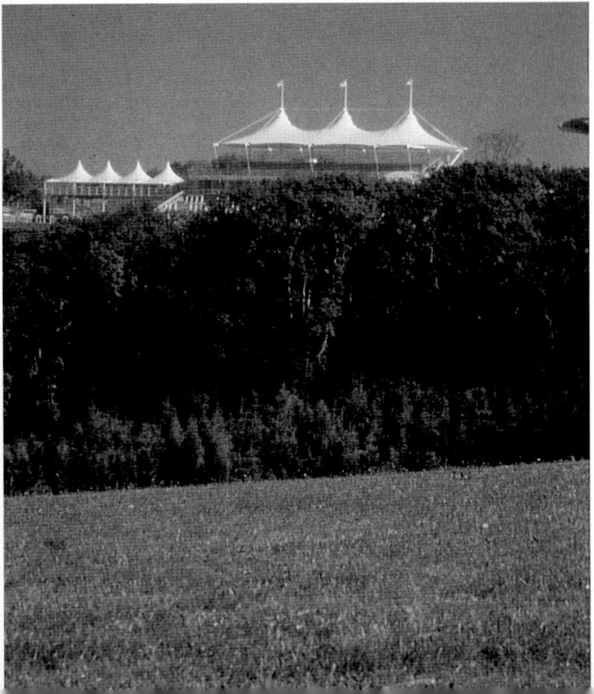

Avenue de Chartres Car Park
Chichester

Probably the largest public building/wall in Chichester apart from the Cathedral. The young architectural firm Birds Portchmouth Russum treated the idea of the car park as an important public building, not just a piece of functional engineering. They set about designing it in such a way that it would catch the attention of visitors to the town, and instill a feeling in ultra-conservative local residents that they too can move with the times. Local press at the opening did not show a particularly positive response to the scheme – 'a Saddamite fortification' – but at least the architects can feel satisfied that they have created a hot architectural debate in an area which is swaddled in conservation bandages. Needless to say, the project received an RIBA Regional Award.

When they won the competition for the building the partners of Birds Portchmouth Russum were all working for Stirling Wilford, and the influences are clear. The use of red brick, a fortification wall, round towers, brightly coloured details and a concern for the context and cohesion with neighbouring buildings (the raised walkways are an extension of the city wall) are all traits to be attributed to the Stirling-Wilford training. They insist that there were neither preconceived ideas about how the building should look nor any attempts to introduce sophisticated technology or composition for the sake of it. There is little expansion on the idea of what a car park might be (customers still have to walk down enclosed stairwells to reach their cars) or what the space might be used for when it is not full of cars, but one would assume that the council is as much to blame for this short sightedness.

Chichester is a catalogue of town-planning blunders and is an example of the way towns, particularly in the south, are heading – one becoming indistinguishable from another. The centre has been pedestrianised to try

West Sussex

Birds Portchmouth Russum 1991

West Sussex

Birds Portchmouth Russum 1991

to maintain picturesque streets, and McDonalds provides the central meeting place, having cunningly moved into an old church hall on the High Street, along with all the usual retailers ... and one wonders why the place feels soulless.

The idea of creating a car park as a new gateway to the city is an interesting one and Avenue de Chartres is without equal. Perhaps it would have been even more interesting if the brief had been developed beyond this one function.

STRUCTURAL ENGINEER Robert Pugh of Ove Arup & Partners
CLIENT Chichester City Council
SIZE 900 car-park spaces
CONTRACT VALUE £5 million
GETTING THERE linked to the town centre by an extension of the city wall on the south side of the town, on the A27
ACCESS open

West Sussex

Birds Portchmouth Russum 1991

West Sussex

Birds Portchmouth Russum 1991

Glyndebourne Opera House

Sir George Christie, son of Glyndebourne founders John and Audrey Christie, had three principle aims when he embarked on this, the first new professional opera house to be built in the Britain since the first version was constructed by his father in 1934. Firstly, the architects and client aimed to create an intimate auditorium, given Glyndebourne's commitment to a repertory policy. Secondly, they aimed to disguise the necessary increase in size of the new building. Thirdly, they aimed to build a theatre without pretensions – to encourage simplicity of style and form without draping it in velvet and gilt.

There were also three principle worries: that the building would be finished on time and within the budget – it was; that the theatre would be an aesthetic and functional disaster – we are all the judges of that; that sufficient funds would be raised – all monies were raised from businesses and individuals in the private sector, highly successfully.

The scenery could not be more quintessentially English. Set in the rolling Sussex Downs, a neo-Elizabethan country house and beautiful gardens are at the heart of Glyndebourne, an opera-going tradition which began in the 1930s and is still today an eccentric experience. Guests in long frocks and dinner jackets enjoy picnicking in the gardens during the hour-long interval. Picnic etiquette and accoutrements have developed (or become more competitive) over the years; they range from the old-fashioned wicker basket and blanket to entire collapsible table arrangements with chandeliers and crystal glasses, some accompanied by butlers. Whatever the weather, revellers continue to dine on the lawn, even in torrential downpours – out come the umbrellas, the Barbour jackets and the stiff upper lips. The new opera house reflects this inveterate resilience – grand in scale and presence but in a practical, brawny way.

The flat-sided oval plan increases the size of the auditorium from 800

East Sussex

Michael Hopkins & Partners 1994

Michael Hopkins & Partners 1994

to 1200 seats and is built on the footprint of the old building. The ground was dug out to reduce the impact of the bulk of the building now nestling between the house, the dressing-room block of the old opera house and the gardens leading across to the car park.

The whole scheme is bound within a single envelope, justified by Hopkins as logical and practical, auditorium, flytower, stage, backstage and wings all relating to the proscenium arch in a symmetrical arrangement – the traditional pattern. The square stage at the centre of the plan is faced by a horseshoe auditorium (a shape established in Italy over 300 years ago) with a semi-circular backstage area. The perimeter of the building houses another layer of activity, three floors of offices and south-facing open foyer balconies (with an unfortunate view of the car park). The benefits of this plan are such that the perimeter rooms form an extra acoustic barrier between inside and outside; it also avoids sheer blank exterior walls, window openings helping to orientate visitors within the building.

The auditorium is a composite structure of concrete and steel surrounded by a load-bearing brick drum – red hand-made Hampshire brick with lime mortar (avoiding unsightly expansion joints). Flat arches between tapered brick piers form the ground foyer arcades. The curved roofs over the auditorium and backstage are lightweight steel-truss structures cantilevering radially from central ring beams, with plywood inner lining and lead cladding on the exterior. The ground-floor foyer area and bar extend beyond the end of the brick drum as a semi-open area sheltered by an illuminated fabric canopy. It is not the formal entrance of the Royal Opera House, but rather more discreetly forms part of the circulation of the opera house, balconies and gardens. The flytower has been the focus of much criticism – which ever way you look at it there is no disguising it!

East Sussex

East Sussex

Michael Hopkins & Partners 1994

Hopkins likens the interior of the auditorium to a musical instrument. The three tiers have a double curved, polished wooden front band (curved in section and plan like a lute), each level having a precise acoustic function. All the walls have vertical wood panelling. The timber is 150-year-old reclaimed pitch pine which not only gives off a mellow smell but makes you feel like you are inside the tree trunk itself. There is no paint, wallpaper, or excessive upholstery (seats are cushioned, the high backs remaining wooden), no carved flourishes.

The success of the scheme, as of so much of Hopkins' work, lies in the unarguably refined method of construction (using many traditional building methods), a sensitive and thorough handling of the materials and understated and immaculately finished details. This makes the difference between architecture and building. As with other Hopkins projects, many of the motifs refer to other projects but have been adapted to suit this particular scheme – see if you can pick them out.

STRUCTURAL ENGINEER Ove Arup & Partners
ACOUSTIC ENGINEER Derek Sugden at Arup Associates
CLIENT Glyndebourne Productions Ltd – Sir George Christie
CONTRACT VALUE £22.6 million
GETTING THERE take the B2192 west out of Lewes on the Ringmer road. Glyndebourne is on a turning to the right before you get to Ringmer
ACCESS open during the festival to ticket holders only

East Sussex

Michael Hopkins & Partners 1994

Michael Hopkins & Partners 1994

Charles Cryer Studio Theatre
Carshalton

The theatre and cinema building was originally a public hall, built in the 1870s (in what is now a conservation area). English Heritage dictated that its building line, ridge line and brickwork remain intact. The needs of modern theatre design meant that the original elements of the structure would not meet new loading requirements. The concrete plank roof, the primary new intervention, had to be heavy so that sound would not be transmitted into or out of the building. A tubular steel structure was introduced to carry loads to the crosswalls at the ends of the auditorium which sit on new foundations. It is one hollow section truss and was made, transported and installed in a single piece. A tubular space frame hangs beneath from which to suspend theatre lighting. A restaurant is concealed within the side of the main building.

Linked by a paved square at the rear of the theatre is the studio theatre and scenery workshop. This is an entirely new building – seemingly inspired by timber barns and hay lofts to achieve the height required to move scenery in and out The hierarchy of structure is defined by colour codings (a familiar trait of this architect) – lattice-trussed columns, gable trusses and cruciform beams clad in timber weatherboarding. The structure looks like a piece of scenery itself.

STRUCTURAL ENGINEER Jampel Davison & Bell
CLIENT London Borough of Sutton
SIZE 700 square metres
CONTRACT VALUE £2.9 million
GETTING THERE High Street, Carshalton
ACCESS open

Surrey

Edward Cullinan Architects 1991

The BRIT School
Thornton Heath, Croydon

This is the first city technology college of its kind, dedicated solely to the teaching of performing arts and related skills. Courses on offer range from set design, to music, food technology, dance, drama, and more. The project was funded by the British Record Industry Trust and the Department of Education and Science.

Fast-track construction meant that the design had to be flexible because changes in the programme would occur and would keep changing once the building was complete as long as the national curriculum continued to move the goal posts. Another determining factor was the necessity to isolate acoustically sensitive areas, such as video, sound and radio broadcasting studios and the auditorium, from the noisier rehearsal rooms and communal areas. The sensitive areas have been embedded into the core of the building which is also the structural core, taking the stresses from four primary trusses anchored by steel anvils at roof level with secondary, fin-shaped trusses hanging from the main ones. The large trusses extend beyond the main structure beneath to accommodate a possible second phase of building work. The external structure produces an entirely column-free double-height space; auditorium/recording studio core with the library sealed in a glazed drum (a glazing system called Reglit) forming a backdrop for the box office in the front lobby, surrounded by the primary circulation route leading on to perimeter classrooms on two floors. External cladding is timber and double-glazed windows for the classrooms and double-height glazed lobbies around the main stair routes (two on both the north and south façades). Daylight and natural ventilation are admitted through roof glazing over the main corridor route on the first floor.

The school requires heavy servicing, particularly given the amount of

Cassidy and Taggart Partnership 1991

Surrey

Cassidy and Taggart Partnership 1991

lights and electronic equipment that it accommodates. Treatment of these details is pragmatic, in keeping with the ethos of the school. Each time a pipe meets the wall it is surrounded by a back-plate, and where the air vents protrude from the glass-walled stair lobbies, the pipework is arranged as a deliberate composition and floor-mounted radiators are on specially designed brackets so that they can be set against glass walls.

From the outside the the structure is logical and discerning but the clarity of the interior has suffered from the curse of all such institutions; posters and banners, shoddy catering facilities and the obligatory make-shift partitions/noticeboards. These can all be found in the main double-height entrance lobby; there is nowhere for students to sit except on the floor or in the bleak dining-room. Surely, if a radiator bracket can be specified, a vital facility/service such as a dining-room deserves equal, if not greater attention.

However, as a city technology college for non-fee-paying students in secondary education, the BRIT School is a rare animal and sets an example that others might emulate and develop in other subjects at this level of the educational ladder. It is also key that it is located in a suburban area when specialist facilities are usually sited in the centre of major cities.

STRUCTURAL ENGINEER Kenchington Ford
CLIENT British Record Industry Trust
SIZE 5300 square metres
CONTRACT VALUE £7,949,000
GETTING THERE follow signs to Selhurst British Rail Station and there will be signs to the BRIT School in The Crescent
ACCESS limited

Surrey

Cassidy and Taggart Partnership 1991

Surrey

Cassidy and Taggart Partnership 1991

Queen's Stand, Epsom Racecourse

Architecturally inspired by a dramatic setting, riding on the crest of a rolling landscape, the stand's perimeter decks or balconies provide (on a clear day) 360° views of the Epsom Downs to the south, Heathrow to the west, Hampstead to the north and Canary Wharf to the east. The stand has a truly celebratory feel as it stands at the race finishing line, especially when stuffed to the gills on Derby Day each June.

The Queen's Stand contains (from the lower ground floor up) jockey facilities, club rooms, bar and dining facilities for up to 5000 members and visitors, the royal suites, privately owned boxes with commentators boxes, photo finish, judges box and television camera platforms in the crow's nest. The elegant stand nextdoor with tiered roof, built in 1829, and a knowledge of the earliest forms of racing facilities (canvas tents and canopies) provided sources for the organisation of facilities in the new stand.

Richard Horden's track record in adapting yacht design to buildings is evident here in terms of materials used: the canopies and roof membrane made from Evalon membrane stuck to plywood and mechanically fixed to steel decking, the aluminium propped mast system, the streamlined nautical fittings in aluminium, and the tough cladding and glass finishes.

STRUCTURAL ENGINEER Ove Arup & Partners
CLIENT United Racecourses Ltd
SIZE 8000 square metres
CONTRACT VALUE £8.5 million
GETTING THERE junction 9 off the M25, follow signs to Epsom, then racecourse along A24
ACCESS free to walk around course, except on Derby Day (June)

Surrey

Richard Horden Associates 1992

Surrey

Richard Horden Associates 1992

London

London

This section describes seven well-known projects and three areas of London that have a high concentration of new building. So, if you only have a day or a weekend to spend in the capital you will be drawn to the key areas of recent architectural interest ... and if you have longer you should buy *London: a guide to recent architecture* which offers more in-depth information.

The section is designed loosely as a tour travelling from west to east across the city, with transport directions between each building so that all, or just part of it can be tackled at any one time. *A–Z London Street Atlas* (standard edition) map co-ordinates are also given in case you are approaching any of the sites from a different direction.

As you cruise on to the Hammersmith flyover, or emerge from Centre West (the traffic island enclosing tube and bus station in the middle of Hammersmith Broadway), the **London Ark** (1991; 5F 75) immediately communicates that it is not just any office block. Designed by Lennart Bergstrom Architects (Ralph Erskine) in association with Rock Townsend Architects, the building readdresses the traditional form of the centrally governed business by creating a working community in which different companies can develop their own identity and contribute to the character of the common social environment contained within the cnetral atrium – 'like a town under a roof'.

The design and construction challenges the conventions of the building services which are often associated with Sick Building Syndrome, making a significant step towards an ecologically sound office building. The tiered interior is flooded with natural light, a fresh-air supply is circulated through the entire space and discharged through ventilators in the timber-lined atrium ceiling and the perimeter is triple glazed to reduce heat loss

Ralph Erskine 1991

Ralph Erskine 1991

and to shhut out traffic noise from the adjacent flyover. The Ark is an environment for living in, not just existing in, providing a welcome alternative to the 1980s' trend of cosmetic rejuvenation.

Take the Piccadilly Line from Hammersmith to Piccadilly Circus or the No. 9 bus to Piccadilly and you will find the Royal Academy of Arts on the north side of Piccadilly. Sandwiched between the Samuel Ware's garden façade (1815) of the original Burlington House (1666) and Sidney Smirke's gallery extension (1867) is a 5-metre wide gap which provides the site for an intervention by Foster Associates – the creation of new circulation up to the previously isolated Diploma Galleries on the third storey, and redesigning these spaces to become The **Sackler Galleries** (1991; 1F 77).

Accessed via the main Royal Academy entrance, a discreet sign points to the galleries to the left of the central stairs. From the atmosphere of a narrow Victorian alley-way at ground level, visitors are rapidly transported by a glass-walled, hydraulic lift up to a new public space. The vertical journey is past three floors of newly renovated façades, reaching a dazzlingly lit sculpture gallery at the summit (illuminated by natural light filtered through translucent glass walls). The sculptures sit along the parapet of Smirke's façade which forms a promenade, crossing a glass bridge, to reach a cool, open ante-room where you can sit and view the Royal Academy's most valuable possession, Michelangelo's 'Virgin and Child with Infant St John'. This series of spaces is simply defined by light and subtle changes in materials, which float structurally independent from the old buildings. The three Diploma Galleries were gutted and rebuilt providing conventional spaces with an improved air quality control system. Visitors can leave the third floor by descending the stair-

London

Foster Associates 1991

case – a combination of grand sweeping stair and fire escape, it winds down through the gap as if walking down into the ground, shadows of footsteps appear above your head through the sand-blasted glass stair treads. The extensive use of different types of glass is a Foster trademark and has filled the ravine with natural light, creating a thrilling new piece of an architectural jigsaw.

A short walk from here to Trafalgar Square, via Piccadilly Circus, taking a left turn at the bottom of the Haymarket, will take you to the **Sainsbury Wing** of the National Gallery (1991; 1H 77) by Venturi, Scott Brown & Associates, Inc. The original scheme for this site took the brunt of the Prince of Wales' irritation with the architectural establishment in 1984 when he condemned it as 'a monstrous carbuncle on the face of a much-loved and elegant friend'. The present scheme was selected in 1986, receiving royal approval.

The new wing houses the collection of early Italian Renaissance and Northern European paintings and temporary exhibitions in 16 daylit galleries, a lecture theatre gallery shop and restaurant, meeting rooms and interactive information centre. The main construction is a steel and concrete frame clad in the same Portland stone as the original building (designed by William Wilkins in 1838). The aesthetics of the building derive from Venturi's postmodern theories of reinterpreting the past by placing it in the present. Many of Wilkins' clasical elements have been reproduced on the new façade and then dissected. Inside, the grand stairway in charcoal black granite has vast arched steel trusses above, mimicking the parts of a coarse Victorian train shed. The gallery spaces symbolise the kinds of 15th-century Tuscan palace rooms in which some of the paintings might have been hung. These are just some of the incon-

London

gruities which lurk suspiciously in the building. Venturi's own words up the project and his attitude towards his architecture: 'it is very sophisticated. You have to be "cultured" to like it.'

On the opposite side of Trafalgar Square, at the top of Whitehall take a no. 77A bus along Millbank to the **Clore Gallery**, at the Tate Gallery (1985; 4J 77) by Stirling Wilford Associates. In 1851, 290 oil paintings and 20,000 works on paper by J M Turner were left to the nation. The daughter of Sir Charles Clore (a friend and benfactor of the Tate Gallery who died before discussions for a new gallery started) proposed that the works be housed under one roof, which gave one of Britain's most outstanding architects an opportunity to design a prominent public building in the capital. The site determined an L-shaped extension, 'a garden building … a bit like an orangery', hence its low roof and attention to landscaping in the foreground. The front façade echoes neighbouring materials – red brick within a honey-coloured stone grid, strikingly windowless except for a bay window, a small arched window and the glazed entrance. You are led across the large entrance hall in a zig-zagging pathway to maximise all areas of the space.

The galleries themselves are conventional in style and proportion. Natural lighting has been a success. Light scoops in the ceiling bounce Thames light on to the walls, making the middle of the gallery slightly darker than the perimeter. When awarded the RIBA National Award in 1988 the jury wrote: ' the rigour with which the rather blandly detailed forms are carried through is commendable'.

Another short walk, turning right on to Millbank (back the way you came), turn left at the roundabout on to Horseferry Road, the road will

Stirling Wilford Associates 1985

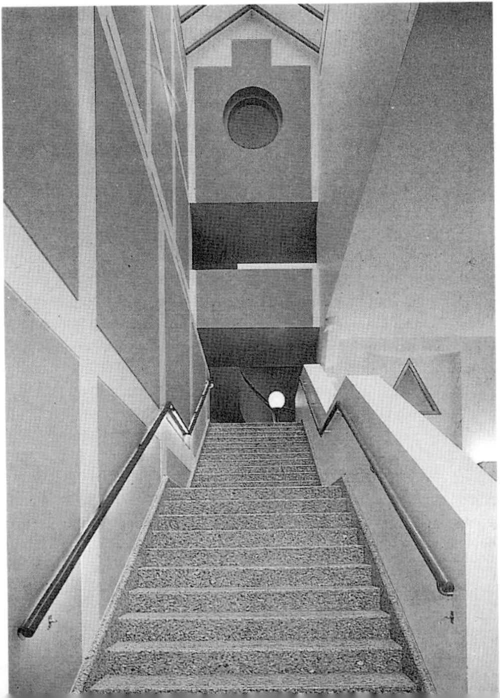

bear around to the right and on your right hand side is the **Channel 4 Headquarters** (1994; 4H 77) designed by the Richard Rogers Partnership (the nearest tube station is St James' Park). This is a key modern building in the heart of Westminster and the first major commission for Sir Richard Rogers in London since the completion of the Lloyd's Building. Situated in a stagnant corner of Victoria (moving out of the Soho/West End media clique), the Channel 4 building will assist in generating a new spirit in the area. The scheme comprises of an underground car park, TV studios and offices, a residential development of 100 apartments (by Lyons Sleeman + Hoare) and a garden square.

In plan there are four wings around a central garden. The north-west sides, forming an L-shaped block, are occupied by Channel 4 , and the south-east blocks are residential. From the staff canteen on the ground floor which opens out onto the garden there is a stark view of the post-modern apartment blocks opposite. The approach to the main entrance is across an elaborate bridge over what appears to be a glass pool but is actually the roof of an underground studio. Conference rooms on the left are stacked in metal-clad boxes slotted into a frame of tapering steel beams. Lifts to the right cling to the service tower and transmission antennae (the feather in the cap). The entrance façade itself is a dramatic concave glass curtain which appears to be draped from a row of curtain claws. Behind this is a series of concrete walkways (above ground floor accessing three floors of offices) punctured by round paving lights.

The entire building is a goldmine of elaborately exaggerated detailing, each individually cast bracket, fixing and cable looks as if it could support the Forth Bridge – if this is the case then I think the structure would have benefitted from a little more restraint. The composition forms a varied low-level landscape rather than a traditional office block.

London

Richard Rogers Partnership 1994

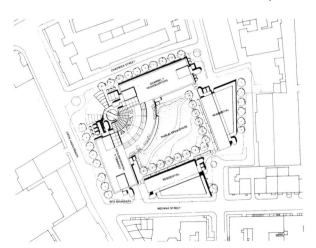

CHADWICK STREET

CHANNEL 4
HEADQUARTERS

RESIDENTIAL

PUBLIC OPEN SPACE

RESIDENTIAL

SITE BOUNDARY

MEDWAY STREET

Richard Rogers Partnership 1994

From the Channel 4 building, walk down Stratton Row (market street), across Victoria Street to St James' Park tube station and take the District and Circle Line to Embankment, changing on to the Northern Line to Waterloo. Up on the main concourse is the **Waterloo International Terminal** (1993; 2K 77) by Nicholas Grimshaw & Partners. This is 'The Gateway to Europe', one of the longest railway stations in the world and the beginning of the three-hour non-stop journey from London to Paris through the Channel Tunnel, which was launched in October 1994 (the inaugral journey was one hour late in departing, in keeping with British Rail tradition). Five new tracks have been laid out which determined the geometry of the whole scheme.

The construction is made up of four components. At the bottom, a reinforced-concrete box forms a car park spanning the underground lines and forming a foundation for the Terminal. Above this is a two-storey viaduct supporting the 400-metre-long platforms. Thirdly, brick vaults beneath the existing station are being repaired to accommodate back-up services. The fourth and most prominent component is the roof, although it comprised only 10 per cent of the £120 million budget. The vast scaly sleeve extends the full length of the platforms, happily disregarding office and apartment blocks along its length, clipping the corners of any building that stands in its way. The complex roof structure is essentially a flattened three-pin bowstring arch, distorted to follow the curve and changing width of the platform. It is clad in a 'loose-fit' glazing system of overlapping standard-size glass sheets linked by concertina joints. Prior to beginning construction on site there was a 16-week dress rehearsal to ensure that everything ran according to plan.

Back on the tube again, take the Northern Line to Kennington, change

Nicholas Grimshaw & Partners 1993

London

Nicholas Grimshaw & Partners 1993

on to the Northern Line (City branch) and go the Monument. Walk up Gracechurch Street, first right on to Fenchurch Street and first left on to Lime Street. You cannot miss the **Lloyd's of London Insurance Market and Offices** (1986; 7E 62) by the Richard Rogers Partnership, probably London's best-known modern building. It is not a tower block – it is rarely perceived as a whole at any one time, but more like a vetical street, with bits of gleaming stainless-steel or electric-blue light at night patched on to the sober City landscape. The unusual configuration is a result of the building's location within the irregular medieval street pattern and the dominant philosophy that the building should appear to be assembled from a 'kit of parts'. All the services cling to the outside of the building, lavatory modules plugged into the sides can feasibly be replaced.

The interior is dominated by a 70-metre-high atrium which is awesomely cathedral-like. Natural light pours down on to the Room (the underwriting room and focus for Lloyd's activities) and additional lighting in the 'omniplatz' office spaces (open-plan, flexible, fully-serviced floors) is supplied by large ceiling fittings which also act as air extractors The triple-glazed external cladding acts as an air duct from ceiling to floor. This building is functionally and aesthetically a living and breathing machine.

The only way to actually see inside is to book in advance for a whole party (071–623 7100) but there is still plenty to see from the outside if you do not make prior arrangements.

The City of London (the capital's financial district) encompasses some of London's oldest buildings as well as new ones. If you continue back up Gracechuch Street becoming Bishopsgate, on your left is Liverpool Street Station and adjacent to this one of the City's largest developments

Richard Rogers Partnership 1986

in recent years, **Broadgate** (1991; 5E 62) by Arup Associates/Skidmore, Owings & Merrill, Inc. In the 1980s there developed an increasing demand for a new type of office space with large floor plates, floor-to-floor heights big enough to accommodate under-floor cabling, flexible spaces which could cope with 24-hour operations and suitable for employees working under highly stressful conditions. The demand was met by the addition of 4.5 million square metres of office space in central London between 1985 and 1991. Broadgate provided some 334,450 square metres (equal to the amount of floor space in five Empire State Buildings). North-American office environments were admired; an impressive facade, lobby with atrium and health club and restaurant facilities to enhance the lives of employees were all transposed to 13 buildings and three squares at Broadgate, focusing around a central arena. In winter it is an ice rink, in summer a stage for concerts. Built into the surrounding pillars, which support offices above and provide shelter around the arena below, are coffee and bagel kiosks. The buildings themselves are unspectacular, mostly steel frame with metal-deck floor construction and external granite cladding, to accommodate anything from an auditorium to a trading floor. Many of the building parts were prefabricated off-site to speed up construction.

One particular building stands out from the rest, **Exchange House**, by Skidmore, Owings & Merrill, Inc, spanning the railway tracks which extend out from Liverpool Street Station. It owes much to bridge technology; four parabolic arches, resting on eight piers support the entire building. The steel-framed box which encloses the office floors hangs between the arches.

It is either a 20-minute walk back down Bishopsgate, left into

Skidmore, Owings & Merrill, Inc 1991

Skidmore, Owings & Merrill, Inc 1991

Houndsditch Street going into Minories Street and across Tower Bridge, or two stops on the tube from Liverpool Street to Tower Hill on the Circle Line and then a five-minue walk over Tower Bridge to the next destination, an area on the left (east) of the south side of Tower Bridge. **Butlers Wharf** (1990; 2F 79), has been subject to a comprehensive revitalisation strategy designed by Conran Roche, to rebuild its infrastructure and restore many of its 17 Grade II listed buildings which were once flour, corn and rice warehouses and then became spice stores. The overall plan is to build a community where people will want to live and work again with leisure , retail, office, residential and industrial facilities. Diverse areas of society are moving in. At one end of Shad Thames is a blue and terracotta painted residential/office/retail development called **Horsley-down Square** (1989) designed by Wickham & Associates, further along students from the London School of Economics live in halls near to luxury apartments and Sir Terence Conran's restaurants and delicatessen. At the eastern end of the site is the **Design Museum** (also set up by Sir Terence Conran and Stephen Bayley) making use of a renovated 1950s' warehouse. Its purpose is to explain the function, appearance and arketing of consumer goods helping to increase awareness of design standards in everything from kettles to cars, from the earliest days of mass-production. The interior spaces were designed by Stanton Williams.

Behind the Design Museum, further along Shad Thames, is the **David Mellor Building** (1990) by Michael Hopkins & Partners, originally built for the cutlery and kitchenware designer and manufacturer but subsequently swallowed up by the Conran Shop empire. The ground floor is occupied by a 3-metre-high glazed shop front set back from a slender columned arcade with workshops and offices on the three floors above with an apartment on the top floor. Services are held in a slate-grey clad

London

Conran Roche 1990

tower adjacent to the main building.

Other projects close by are two schemes by czwg: **The Circle** (1989), Queen Elizabeth Street, and **China Wharf** (1988), Mill Street, and an interesting building built on a very tight budget (£350,000) called **Camera Press** (1993) by Panter Hudspith, Queen Elizabeth Street.

The final leg of your trip takes you right out to the Docklands and **Canary Wharf** (1991; 1D 80). Take the Docklands Light Railway, the station is near to Tower Hill, directly to Canary Wharf (there is a limited service at night). There are several major projects in and around the Isle of Dogs, notably the **Financial Times Print Works** (1988; 6C 64) by Nicholas Grimshaw & Partners and a **Control Centre and Lifting Bridges** (1990; 1E 80) by Alsop Lyall & Störmer which you will see on the eastern acces road out of Canary Wharf. Canary Wharf itself was masterplanned by the American firm, Skidmore, Owings & Merrill, Inc. The late Francis Tibbalds, writing in *The Architects' Journal* (7 November 1990), sums up Europe's largest single development: 'If you want to see what, left to its own devices, the private sector produces, one need look no further than the Isle of Dogs in London's Docklands. The British Government's flagship of "enterprise culture development" and urban design challenge of the century adds up to little more than market-led, opportunistic chaos – an architectural circus ... Sadly, there was a necessary intermediate step betwen balance sheet and buildings that got missed in the rush. It is called urban design.'

The landmark at the centre of all of this is the tower above Cabot Square by Cesar Pelli & Associates, its most interesting aspect being that it is the first skyscraper to be clad in stainless steel. The tower was originally to be another five floors higher but the London Docklands Devel-

Panter Hudspith 1993

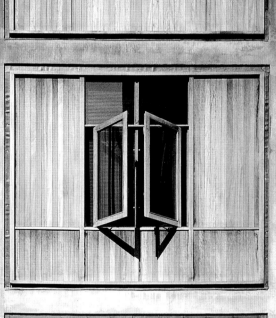

opment Corporation laid down rigid rules about sizes of floor plans and heights. Subsequent buildings have all been effected by these harsh guidelines, producing a bland, impenetrable corporate image throughout. Other buildings on the site have been designed by Pei, Cobb, Freed & Partners, Kohn Pederson Fox and Troughton McAslan but one is barely distinguishable from another. Due to intense security measures (there was a terrorist bomb attempt on the tower in 1991), the area is taking a long time to evolve a life of its own, hampered by poor transport connections to and from site. However, roads links are improving and companies such as the Mirror Group have moved out there. Also, it will be the new headquarters for London's first cable channel, Network 1, so the physical connection with Canary Wharf might not be strong but the information highway should make it more accessible in the future.

London

Nicholas Grimshaw & Partners 1988

London

Nicholas Grimshaw & Partners 1988

Index

England: a guide to recent architecture

England: a guide to recent architecture

England: a guide to recent architecture

England: a guide to recent architecture

England: a guide to recent architecture

England: a guide to recent architecture

England: a guide to recent architecture

England: a guide to recent architecture

England: a guide to recent architecture

England: a guide to recent architecture

England: a guide to recent architecture

England: a guide to recent architecture

England: a guide to recent architecture

England: a guide to recent architecture

London
A guide to recent architecture

Despite the tackiness of many of the buildings spawned during the 1980s' financial boom and the contraction of opportunity resulting from the subsequent recession, a lot of good architecture has been built in London during the last decade. This book, a 1994 AIA award winner, describes and comments on a hundred projects from this period, covering all the best, a few of the worst, and the interesting.

The range of building types covered includes major public projects – Nicholas Grimshaw's Waterloo International Terminal, pumping stations by Richard Rogers and John Outram, a new headquarters for MI6, schools and hospitals – private houses, offices, shops, bars and restaurants. The Broadgate office development demonstrates a sophisticated and successful urbansim largely missing from other commercial projects from this period, while a self-build scheme for adults with learning difficulties shows the potential of 'community architecture' for inner-city rejuvenation.

As architecture in London starts to move away from style-based issues and towards a more environmentally responsible and humanistic agenda, this book charts the changes and provides a critical record of an adventurous decade.

- 320 pages
- 150 illustrations

Samanthan Hardingham

:

Samanthan Hardingham

Chicago
A guide to recent architecture

The 'home of the skyscraper', inheritor of the legacy of Frank Lloyd Wright and the Prairie School, and one of the most important sites of Mies van der Rohe's pioneering Modernism, Chicago has been at the forefront of architecture for the last century. This book, which describes and illustrates exactly one hundred buildings of the last ten years, chronicles the current architecture scene, covering the work of established firms and the new, up-and-coming design stars.

The buildings included represent a cross section in terms of size and function – from the giant office blocks of the Loop to single-family houses and municipal facilities in the suburbs. The monuments of the speculative skyscraper boom of the early 1980s are well represented, but this is a phase that has ground to a halt, and interesting work is now seen in such public projects as the giant and controversial Harold Washington Library, or the Cesar Chavez Elementary School, a new facility in a less-than-affluent part of the city.

Many of Chicago's new buildings are the products of a reactionary historicist vogue, but new and daring work is being built, such as Bertrand Goldberg's River City development, or the Peter Elliott Studios, a gem in a predominantly mundane industrial neighbourhood. Chicago is also the home of international institutions Playboy and McDonalds whose headquarters and training centre (Hamburger University, complete with McNature Trail and Lake Fred) respectively are described here.

320 pages
150 illustrations

Susanna Sirefman

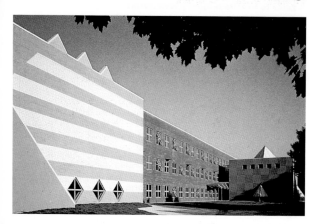

Susanna Sirefman

Prague
A guide to twentieth-century architecture

Prague is an overwhelming city: buildings from many periods are arranged like theatrical scenery, modern, hard-edged structures mingle with soft Baroque or Secessionist façades, towers and spires are silhouetted against a backdrop of wavy, red-tiled roofs. This book explores twentieth–century Prague, selecting some 120 buildings from perhaps 1500 of architectural interest.

Among the buildings described and illustrated are major works by Adolf Loos (the Villa Müller is one of less-well-known architectural treasures of the century), Jose Plecnik (the Church of the Sacred Heart is perhaps his masterpiece), and Bruno Paul. Unique to Prague is the Cubist style, seen in many buildings including Josef Chochol's spectacular Hodek Apartments of 1913 and the slightly earlier Villa Kovarovic. Prague was also a cradle of Modernism, with buildings by Ladislav Zak, Mart Stam, Otokar Novotny, and many other pioneers of the movement. Finally, the Prague guide includes some curiosities: the first building by Future System's Jan Kaplicky, Franz Kafka's Cubist tombstone, a Cubist lamp-post.

An introduction provides the historical and cultural information necessary for an understanding of the city, and biographies of Prague architects are provided.

- 320 pages
- 160 illustrations

Ivan Margolius

Ivan Margolius

:

Los Angeles
A guide to recent architecture

The current image of Los Angeles architecture has been largely shaped by books, magazines and exhibitions that focus on the work of the 'LA School', represented most famously by architects such as Frank O. Gehry, and Morphosis, and by that of a younger generation that includes Michele Saee, O'Herlihy + Warner and studio bau:ton. At its best the style is characterised by strong buildings with unexpected juxtapositions, disrupted forms, the inventive use of industrial materials, and detailing with the finesse of jewellery. The LA School is well represented in the Los Angeles guide, but it also covers the modernism of architects such as Raymond Kappe and Pierre Koenig, the post-modernism of Charles Moore and the rationalism of Charles Ward.

Somewhat surprisingly, the decade covered here has seen some rediscovery of Los Angeles' tradition of public spaces. Examples include the 3rd Street Promenade in Santa Monica, the sadly compromised Beverly Hills Civic Center, and Pershing Square. World-class architects have found patrons in the city – Michael Eisner at Walt Disney has commissioned buildings by Michael Graves, Robert M. Stern and Venturi Scott Brown; Frederick Norton Smith is employing Eric Moss as he develops Culver City; Richard Meier is building the new Getty Center.

The Los Angeles guide describes more than one hundred buildings, giving a picture of the range and achievements of architecture in the city.

. 320 pages
. 150 illustrations

Dian Phillips-Pulverman

Dian Phillips-Pulverman

Photographs

All photographs are by Susan Benn except:
pages 25, 27: FaulknerBrowns
pages 47, 49: Jeremy Dixon . Edward Jones
pages 51, 53: John Lyall Architects
page 59: Edward Cullinan Architects
pages 93, 95: Arcaid
pages 101, 103, Studio BAAD, Jeremy Cockayne
pages 163, 165: Jonathan Ellis-Miller Architects
page 199: Foster Associates
page 241: Terry Farrell Partnership, Richard Bryant
page 275: David Chipperfield Architects, Richard Bryant